LINZ

Tradition · Moderne · Vision
Tradition and Modern Vision

Text von Christoph Wagner

Mit 160 Farbbildern nach Photographien von Ali Andreß,
Franz Hubmann, Peter Peter u. a.

Herausgegeben von Joachim Klinger

Übersetzt von Michael Bull

Text by Christoph Wagner

*160 colour illustrations from photographs by Ali Andreß,
Franz Hubmann, Peter Peter et al.*

Edited by Joachim Klinger

Translated by Michael Bull

Verlag Christian Brandstätter

INHALT

Oben: Dreifaltigkeitssäule mit Pöstlingberg.
Above: Holy Trinity Column with Pöstlingberg.
Mitte: Martinskirche.
Middle: St. Martin's Church.
Unten: Laubenhof des Landhauses.
Below: Courtyard of the Provincial Administration.

TABLE OF CONTENTS

Oben: Design Center.
Above: Design Center.
Mitte: Neues Rathaus.
Middle: New City Hall.
Unten: Eine Anlage der OMV-Gruppe.
Below: OMV Group plant.

Die VOEST-Brücke ist der modernste Verkehrsträger über die Donau.

LINZ

Der augenfälligste Vorzug von Linz ist das land-
schaftliche Umfeld. Die Donau betritt das Linzer
Becken in einem besonders romantischen
Durchbruch zwischen dem idyllischen Pöstlingberg und dem geheimnisvoll-düsteren Kürnberger Wald. Der Nibelungenstrom ist seit jeher die
eigentliche Lebensader der Linzer gewesen.
Bleiben wir gleich bei der Historie. Das Römer-
kastell Lentia wurde um 410 n. Chr. erstmals
erwähnt. Zu Beginn des 10. Jahrhunderts
besitzt Linz das Marktrecht. Im 13. Jahrhundert
erhält Linz Stadtcharakter und 1458 wird es zur
fürstlichen Residenz. Als Kaiser Friedrich III.
zwischen 1489 und 1493 von Linz aus das Reich
regiert, steht die Stadt im Mittelpunkt der
Politik. Aber auch nachher laufen die Fäden der
Geschichte hier immer wieder zusammen.
Seit in Linz 1672 die erste Textilmanufaktur
Mitteleuropas und 1832 die erste Pferdeeisenbahn des Kontinents eröffnet wurden, hat es sich
einen weltweiten Ruf als Zentrum von Handel,
Industrie und technischem Fortschritt erobert.
Und Linz bietet eine ungebrochene kulturelle
Tradition. Die Stadt Johannes Keplers, Adalbert
Stifters und Anton Bruckners verdankt ihr inter-
nationales Ansehen nicht zuletzt ihrer lebendi-
gen Kulturszene zwischen Brucknerfest, Ars
Electronica und Pflasterspektakel.
Mit 200.000 Einwohnern ist die oberösterrei-
chische Landeshauptstadt die drittgrößte Stadt
Österreichs. Ihre flächenmäßige Ausdehnung
beträgt 96,1 km².

The VOEST Bridge is the most modern traffic artery over the Danube.

LINZ

The most striking advantage of Linz is the countryside in her surroundings. The Danube flows into the Linz basin at an especially romantic point between idyllic Pöstlingberg and the dark, mysterious Kürnberger Wald. The great river of the Nibelungs has always been the scenic, historical and economic lifeline of Linz.

Let's look at the history of the place for a moment. In 410 B.C. the Roman castellum Lentia was first documented. At the beginning of the 10th century Linz received the right to hold markets. In the 13th century Linz took on the character of a city and 1458 it became a princely residence. The city became the centre of political activity between the years 1489 and 1493 when Emperor Friedrich III governed the empire from Linz. But even after such significant events, Linz has remained the focus point for many threads of historical development. After having been the site of the first textile factory in central Europe in 1672 and the first horse-drawn railway of the continent in 1832, Linz has gone on to gain a worldwide reputation as a centre of trade, industry and technical progress.

Linz has an unbroken cultural tradition. The city of Johannes Kepler, Adalbert Stifter und Anton Bruckner has earned an international reputation thanks to its lively cultural life which ranges from the Bruckner Festival to Ars Electronica and the Sidewalk Spectacle.

With 200.000 residents the provincial capital of Upper Austria is also Austria's third largest city. It's area comprises 96.1 km².

5

HERRSCHAFTLICHES LINZ
Stately Linz

Der Turm des Linzer Landhauses.
The Tower of the Linz Provincial Administration.
Gegenüberliegende Seite: Blick vom Urfahrer Brückenkopf auf die Altstadt.
Opposite page: View of the Old Town from Urfahrer Brückenkopf.

7

Das Schloß: Zwischen Residenz und Kaserne

Auf den ersten Blick sieht das Linzer *Schloß* wie ein überdimensionaler Vierkanthof aus, der sich irrtümlich auf eine Anhöhe über dem Donaustrom verirrt hat. Dabei enthält es, wenn man in der Schloßgeschichte nachliest, so ziemlich alle Ingredienzien eines Machtzentrums, das zeitweise sogar der Wiener Hofburg den Rang abgelaufen hat. Schon 799 wird eine „Burg in Linz" erwähnt.

In den Jahren 1489 bis 1493 ist das Linzer Schloß unter Friedrich III. das Zentrum des Heiligen Römischen Reiches Deutscher Nation. Unter Kaiser Rudolf II. wurde die Burg mit ihren noch recht mittelalterlichen Bastionen und Vorwerken weiter ausgebaut, woran nicht zuletzt die Linzer Landstände Schuld waren. Sie hatten, um ihre Macht zu betonen, dem eher armselig wirkenden Schloß den Prunkbau des Linzer Landhauses entgegengesetzt. Was blieb dem Kaiser also anderes übrig, als seinen Machtanspruch durch einen weiteren Schloßtrakt zu untermauern? Der heutigen Schloßanlage würde man soviel Trutzigkeit nicht mehr ansehen. Sie ist freilich auch nur mehr ein Überbleibsel einstiger Pracht. Der Linzer Großbrand im Jahre 1800 hatte den mächtigen Südtrakt völlig zerstört, der nie wieder erneuert wurde. Heute betritt man das

The Castle: Residence and Barracks

At first glance, the Castle at Linz looks like an overdimensional four-sided farmhouse, which strayed by mistake to a vantage point above the Danube. And yet, if you delve deeply into the castle chronicle, you will find every component of a true centre of power, one which even supersed the Winter Palace in Vienna for a time. In 799 a "castle in Linz" is first mentioned.

From 1489 to 1493 the castle became the centre of the holy Roman Empire under Friedrich III. Under Emperor II, the Castle, which at this time still retained its medieval bastions and gables, was further extended, a decision for which the local estates of the realm were partly responsible. In order to emphasize their power, they erected a magnificent administrative seat called the Assembly House in visual contrast to the rather unprepossessing abode of the emperor. What other choice could he make but to strengthen his show of power by building yet another wing to the castle?

It is hard to imagine so much defiance in the face of its present appearance. It is, of course, only a remnant of its former glory. A conflagration in 1800 destroyed the monumental south wing entirely and it was never rebuilt. Today, the visitor

Das Urfahrer Steinmetzplatzl, im Hintergrund das Linzer Schloß.
The Urfahrer Steinmetzplatzl, in the background, the Castle of Linz.

Trakt des ehemaligen kaiserlichen Schlosses.
Wing of the former Imperial Palace.

Schloß, das von 1811–1851 als Gefängnis und bis in die Nachkriegszeit tatsächlich als Kaserne diente, durch das Rudolfstor, nach dem Schloßhof gelangt man dann zum alten Friedrichsbau mit dem Friedrichstor, über dessen Spitzbogen ein alter Wappenstein mit der Jahreszahl 1481 angebracht ist, der den Wahlspruch Kaiser Friedrichs trägt:
A E I O U – „Alles Erdreich ist Österreich untertan."
Nach einer vollständigen Restaurierung hat das Linzer Schloß seit 1963 eine neue Bestimmung gefunden. In seinen Räumen ist das *Linzer Schloßmuseum*, ein Teil des Oberösterreichischen Landesmuseums, untergebracht. Schwerpunkt sind neben ur- und frühgeschichtlichen Sammlungen vor allem kunstgeschichtliche und volkskundliche Exponate wie der Eggelsberger Flügelaltar – Kultur und Geschichte des Landes Oberösterreich werden hier lebendig gehalten.

enters the Castle, which served as a prison from 1811 to 1851 and then as a barracks until the post war era, through the Rudolf gate, behind the castle couryard, one reaches the older section dating back to Friedrich's time with its Friedrich Gate. Here, above the lancet, is an old coat of arms with the date 1481 bearing the slogan of Emperor Friedrich:
A E I O U – "Alles Erdreich ist Österreich untertan" meaning "All the world is a Vassal of Austria".
After its thorough restoration in 1963, the Castle of Linz has found a new function. The Linzer Schlossmuseum, *a castle museum, is now located in its rooms and it contains a part of the collections of the Upper Austria Provincial Museum. The emphasis, aside from collections of pre- and ancient history, is on art history and folklore exhibits such as the Eggelberg Triptychon, all of which keep the culture and history of Austria truly alive.*

Oben links: In den Schloßberganlagen. – Above left: In the park of the Castle Hill.
Oben rechts: Linzer Schloß. Tor mit dem Wappen Kaiser Friedrichs III. – Above right: The Castle of Linz. Gate with the arms of Emperor Friedrich III.
Unten links: Florianerstube im Schloßmuseum. – Below left: St. Florian Room in the castle museum.
Unten rechts: Gang im Schloßmuseum mit spätgotischen und Renaissance-Plastiken. – Below right: Corridor in the castle museum with late-gothic and renaissance sculptures.

Johannes-Kepler-Denkmal auf dem Schloßberg.
Johannes Kepler Monument on the Castle Hill.

Blick auf Linz an der Donau. – View of Linz on the Danube.

Landhaus. Laubenhof mit dem Planetenbrunnen. – The Provincial Administration. Garden courtyard with Planet Fountain.
Gegenüberliegende Seite: Der Turm des Landhauses. – Opposite page: The tower of the Provincial Administration.

Stände mit Steherqualitäten:
Das Linzer Landhaus

Zu den Sternen konnten die mächtigen Stände des Landes ob der Enns – die Prälaten, die Herren, die Ritter und die landesfürstlichen Städte – im 16. Jahrhundert noch nicht greifen. Aber hoch hinaus wollten sie allemal. Vielleicht ist das auch ein Grund, warum im *Arkadenhof*, einem der schönsten Renaissance-Innenhöfe Österreichs, ausgerechnet ein Planetenbrunnen steht. Geschaffen hat ihn der Linzer Steinmetz Peter Guet im Jahre 1582. Man muß schon genauer hinsehen, um die Zeichen- und Formensprache dieses manieristischen Kunstwerks zu verstehen. Daß hier Fixsterne, Mond und Planeten wild durcheinandergewirbelt wurden, hat die Linzer auch später nicht gestört. Immerhin entdeckte Johannes Kepler, der in der im *Landhaus* untergebrachten Ständeschule unterrichtete, nur

The Defiant Estates:
The Assembly House of Linz

The powerful estates of the realm at home above the river Enns, that is, the prelates, the gentry and the knights of the area, could not yet reach for the stars in the 16th century. But they were indeed ambitious. Perhaps this is the very reason that the arcaded courtyard, one of the most beautiful Renaissance courtyards of Austria, is the site of a planetary fountain. A local stonemason, Peter Guet, finished it in the year 1582. It is necessary to look closely in order to understand the symbolic language of this manneristic work of art. It has never bothered the people of Linz that the fixed stars, moon and planets are all scattered about in utter confusion. After all, Johannes Kepler himself taught at the school which was located in the Assembly House, *but he discovered the third planetary law a few decades after the completion of*

Landhaus. Nordportal mit Wappen.
Provincial Administration. North portal with coats of arms.

wenige Jahrzehnte nach Fertigstellung des Brunnens das dritte Planetengesetz. Wichtiger als die wissenschaftliche Wahrheit war den Ständen allerdings, daß ihr Prunkbau das kaiserliche Schloß oben auf der Anhöhe in den Schatten stellte. Man wollte dem Kaiser möglichst symbolkräftig mitteilen, wer ob der Enns das Sagen hatte. Aus diesem Grund versah man das Gebäude, wie wir heute sagen würden, mit dem letzten Zeitgeist-Chic. Und der kam damals nun einmal aus dem Italien der Renaissance. Als Baumeister für das Linzer Landhaus wurde dann auch Christoph Canevale bestellt. Das prunkvolle Tor an der Nordfront, das mit jenem von Porcia und dem Schweizertor der Wiener Hofburg zu den schönsten seiner Art in Österreich zählt, schuf der Venezianer Kaspar Toretto. Das Innere des Landhauses wird vom berühmten „Steinernen Saal" beherrscht, in dem früher die Landstände zusammentraten. Heute tagt die Landesregierung im 1863 entstandenen neuen Landtagssaal.

the fountain. To the estates of the realm, however, the fact that their magnificent new Assembly House put the Imperial Castle on the hill into the shade was a great deal more important than scientific accuracy. It was a pointed attempt to let the emperor know, with the help of meaningful symbols, just who held the real power in the region above the Enns. That is the reason that the building was conceived as a reflection of the very latest "Zeitgeist-Chic" as we might put it today. In those days, the latest architectural fashion came from the Italy of the Renaissance. Christoph Canevale was comissioned as master builder of the Assembly House. The Venetian Kaspar Toretto was responsible for the magnificent gate on the north front which, together with the one of Porcia and the Swiss Gate of the Vienna Hofburg, is among the most beautiful in Austria. The interior of the Assembly House is dominated by the famous "Stone Hall" in which the diet sat in former times. Today, the provincial government meets in the new Parliament Hall of 1863.

Die Wohnung des Bischofs

Der Bischofshof, der heute als bedeutendster barocker Profanbau von Linz gilt, war ursprünglich im Auftrag der Äbte des Stifts Kremsmünster erbaut worden. Sie standen traditionell an der Spitze der Prälatenriege im Landtag, zu dem es von ihrem „Vierkanter" in der Herrenstraße nur ein Katzensprung war. Den neuen Bischofshof hat Josef II. indessen nicht einfach requiriert, sondern den Kremsmünsterern ordnungsgemäß abgekauft. Sie erwarben mit dem Geld eine neue Liegenschaft: den „Klosterhof", nunmehr ein bekanntes Bierlokal an der Linzer Landstraße. Seine Bedeutung verdankt der Bischofshof vor allem dem Baumeister, der ihn geschaffen hat, handelt es sich dabei doch um keinen Geringeren als den Erbauer der Stifte Melk und St. Florian, Jakob Prandtauer.

The Apartment of the Bishop

The Episcopal Residence, or Bischofshof, is today considered the most significant secular building of Linz and was originally built for the Monastery of Kremsmünster. They were traditionally at the forefront of the Assembly of Prelates at the diet which met only a stone's throw from their great square residence in Herrenstrasse. But Josef II did not, in fact, simply requisition the new Episcopal Residence, but quite officially purchased it from the Kremsmünster Abbots. With the proceeds, they purchased a new property, the so-called "Klosterhof", which houses a beer hall in Linzer Landstrasse today. The true significance of the Episcopal Residence lies in its builder, none other than the creator of the monasteries at Melk and St. Florian, Jakob Prandtauer.

Der Bischofshof, nach Entwurf von Jakob Prandtauer erbaut, im Hintergrund der „Neue Dom".
The Bishop's Courtyard, built after plans by Jakob Prandtauer, in the background, the "New Cathedral".

RELIGIÖSES
LINZ
Religious Linz

„Alter Dom" (Jesuitenkirche). Blick in das reichgeschmückte Innere.
"Old Cathedral" (Church of the Jesuits). View of the ornate interior.
Gegenüberliegende Seite: Blick auf den „Alten Dom".
Opposite page: View of the Old Cathedral.

Fassade der Martinskirche. – Facade of St. Martin's Church.

In Österreichs ältester Kirche

Es strömt nur wenig Licht durch die Fenster aus der Karolingerzeit. Der schlichte, einschiffige Kirchenraum macht unter der roh gezimmerten Holzdecke einen kargen, ganz und gar unspektakulären Eindruck. Dennoch war die *Martinskirche*, als man sie nach dem Zweiten Weltkrieg renovierte und dabei auf die Fundamente eines Baues aus der Römerzeit stieß, eine echte Sensation. Das brüchige Gemäuer atmet noch die Aufbruchsstimmung des frühen Christentums. Das damalige Karolingerreich ist auch jene Zeit, in welcher der Name Linz, oder genauer „Linze", zum ersten Mal erwähnt wird.

Jahrhundertelang wußten die Linzer gar nicht,

In Austria's Oldest Church

Only a little light comes through the window of the old church from the Carolingian period. The simple, single-nave interior makes a barren, entirely unspectacular impression with its roughly fashioned wooden ceiling. Nevertheless, the Martinskirche, St. Martin's Church, became a country-wide sensation when it was renovated after the Second World War and the fountain was discovered to date back to Roman times, making it one of the oldest churches in all Austria. The cracked walls still exhale the spirit of turmoil which earmarked early Christianity. By the way, the Carolingian Empire is the time when the name Linz, or to be exact "Linze", was used first.

Innenraum der Martinskirche. – Interior of St. Martin's Church.

welchen Schatz sie da in einem stillen Winkel des alten Römerbergs hüteten. Zeitweise diente das Martinskirchlein eher profanen Zwecken. Bei der Wiederherstellung im Jahre 1947 wurde übrigens auch ein wertvoller Kunstschatz gefunden: Das freigelegte Al-Secco-Gemälde stammt aus dem frühen 15. Jahrhundert und ist eine Nachbildung jenes berühmten Volto-Santo-Bildes aus dem italienischen Wallfahrtsort Lucca, welches das Antlitz des Erlösers zeigt. Das Bild befindet sich heute an der Nordwand der Kirche und stellt – neben ein paar Resten gotischer Ausmalung – eines der raren farbigen Elemente dieses durch naive Einfachheit bestechenden Gotteshauses dar.

The people of Linz were unaware for centuries of the treasure lying in a quiet corner of the old Roman hill. At times it was even used for secular purposes. During its renovation in 1947, a valuable art treasure was discovered: an al-secco-painting from the early 15th century was found beneath the plaster and restored. It is a copy of the famous Volto-Santo painting in the Italian pilgrimage town of Lucca and shows the face of the Saviour. The painting can be seen on the north wall of the church and represents, together with a few fragments of Gothic ornamentation, one of the few touches of colour in this church of striking simplicity.

Der „Alte Dom"

Als um 1600 die ersten Jesuiten nach Linz kamen, ahnten sie noch nicht, daß die fast ein dreiviertel Jahrhundert später fertiggestellte *Jesuitenkirche* dereinst insgesamt sieben Bischöfen 147 Jahre hindurch als Domkirche dienen sollte.

Die wahre Größe des vermutlich vom italienischen Architekten Pietro Francesco Carlone geschaffenen Monumentalbaus ermißt man am besten, wenn man die beiden majestätischen Türme vom Hauptplatz aus betrachtet, denn in der engen Häuserschlucht der Domgasse kann die prachtvolle Fassade ihre eindrucksvolle Wirkung keineswegs entfalten.

An der Domorgel, einem „Beutestück" aus Engelszell, wirkte Anton Bruckner, der hier auch seine d-Moll-Messe uraufführte, zwölf Jahre lang als Linzer Domorganist. Als mit der Industrialisierung im 19. Jahrhundert auch die Bevölkerung von Linz stetig wuchs, schien der „Alte Dom" Bischof Rudigier bald zu klein. Der neugotische Maria-Empfängnis-Dom wurde in Auftrag gegeben. Doch die Bauarbeiten zogen sich jahrzehntelang hin. Und so schrieb man das Jahr 1909, als das Domkapitel zum letzten Mal in der Jesuitenkirche, die seither wieder dem Orden gehört, der Vesperandacht beiwohnte.

Oben: Die Dreifaltigkeitssäule und der „Alte Dom". – Above: The Holy Trinity Column and the "Old Cathedral".
Unten: Blick auf den neugotischen Maria-Empfängnis-Dom. – Below: View of the neo-gothic Maria Emfängnis Dom.

The "Alte Dom" – the Old Cathedral

When the first Jesuits came to Linz around 1600, they did not yet realize that the Jesuit Church which would be finished three quarters of a century later would serve as a cathedral for 147 years under the guidance of seven bishops.

The true grandeur of this monumental building by the Italian architect Pietro Francesco Carlone can best be appreciated if both the majestic towers are viewed from the Main Square. From the narrow lane called Domgasse however, the impressive effect of the magnificent facade cannot be seen in all complexity.

The organ which was "looted" from Engelszell, was played by Anton Pruckner, who played the first performance of his D-minor Mass here, during his twelve years as cathedral organist. When the population of Linz grew in the 19th century, the so-called "old cathedral" seemed much too small to its current bishop, Rudiger. The neo-gothic Maria-Empfängnis-Dom was commissioned. But the construction lasted for decades. It was not until 1909 that the last evening vespers were read in the Jesuit Church: it was then returned to the original order.

Gegenüberliegende Seite: Der mächtige Innenraum des „Neuen Domes". – Opposite page: The magnificent interior of the "New Cathedral".

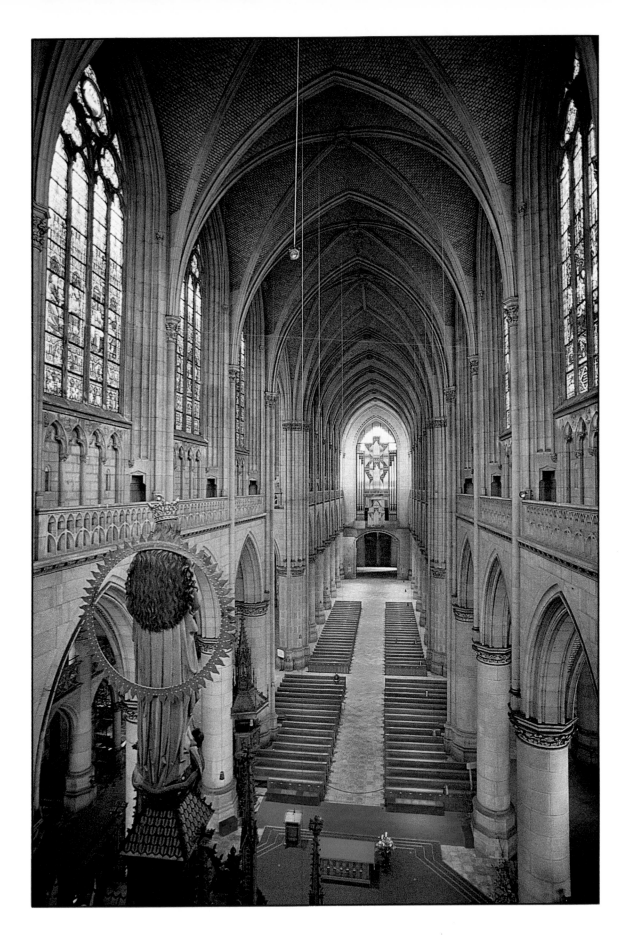

Der „Neue Dom"

Der Linzer Dom ist eine so perfekte Nachbildung gotischer Bauweise, daß es schon eines sehr kritischen Blickes bedarf, um ihn als ein Kind des 19. Jahrhunderts zu entlarven. Was die Größenverhältnisse betrifft, so hat sich Dombaumeister Vinzenz Statz nämlich exakt an die Faustregeln seiner mittelalterlichen Vorfahren gehalten. Etwa an jene, die besagt, daß ein gotischer Dom ungefähr gleich lang sein müsse wie der Turm hoch. Als im Jahr 1862 der Grundstein für das neue Gotteshaus gelegt wurde, zählte Linz 27.000 Einwohner, das sind nur um 7.000 mehr, als schließlich der endgültige Fassungsraum des Domes betragen sollte. Daß Linz den höchsten Kirchturm Österreichs bekam, scheiterte nur am Einspruch der Wiener, die eine Höhe knapp unter jener des Stephansturms vorschrieben. In jüngster Zeit hat man dem Linzer Dom eine weitere Attraktion hinzugefügt: Die von der dänischen Orgelbaufirma Marcussen gebaute Rudigier-Orgel, die 1968 eingeweiht wurde, zählt zu den größten, schönsten und wohlklingendsten Orgeln Europas.

The "Neue Dom" – the New Cathedral

The Cathedral of Linz is such a perfect interpretation of Gothic building style that it requires a highly critical eye to discover its origins as a child of the 19th century. In respect to its dimensions, the cathedral master builder Vinzenz Statz kept to all the rules of thumb observed by his medieval ancestors. Especially that one which holds that a gothic cathedral should be the same length as the height of its tower. When the cornerstone for the new church was laid in 1862, Linz had a population of 27,000 inhabitants and that was just 7,000 more than the capacity of the intended building. Linz only just missed having the highest church tower in Austria owing to protests from Vienna which prescribed a height just slightly less than St. Stephan's. In recent times, the Cathedral of Linz has gained yet another distinction: the Rudigier-Organ, built by the Danish organ makers Marcussen, was consecrated in 1968 and numbers among the largest, most beautiful and perfectly balanced organs in Europe.

Dieser Kirche gehört das Herz des Kaisers

Kaiser Friedrich III. hat sein Herz nämlich in jener Kirche gelassen, der es Zeit seines Lebens gehört hat: in der Linzer *Stadtpfarrkirche*, der zweitältesten Kirche von Linz. Dort ruhen Herz und Eingeweide des Kaisers hinter einem Wappenstein rechts vom Hochaltar. Am interessantesten ist die Kirche vielleicht von außen. Wo heute der Linzer Großstadtverkehr in willkommene Parkplätze rund um das Gotteshaus mündet, befand sich nämlich früher ein Friedhof. Von ihm stammen zahlreiche der heute in die Außenmauern eingelassenen gotischen und barocken Marmorgrabsteine.

Gegenüberliegende Seite: Der neugestaltete Park um den „Neuen Dom".
Opposite page: The newly-laid out park and the "New Cathedral".
Rechts : Durchblick auf den Turm der Stadtpfarrkirche.
Right: View of the tower of the City Parish Church.
Unten: Stadtpfarrkirche. Detail eines Grabdenkmals.
Below: City Parish Church. Detail from a gravestone.

The Heart of the Emperor Belongs to this Church

Emperor Friedrich III left his heart to the church which had claimed his affections in life, the Stadtpfarrkirche, *or Parish Church of Linz, the second oldest church in town. The heart and entrails of the emperor rest behind a stone coat of arms to the right of the High Altar. Perhaps the exterior of the church is most interesting of all. A graveyard used to be situated just here where the city traffic of Linz tries to find a coveted parking place somewhere around the church. The gothic and baroque marble headstones of this graveyard may be seen today embedded in the outside walls of the church.*

Das Landeskulturzentrum Ursulinenhof mit den Türmen der Ursulinenkirche.
The Provincial Culture Centre in the Ursulinenhof
with the towers of the Church of the Ursulines.

Fassade der Barmherzigen-Brüder-Kirche. – Facade of the Barmherzigen Brüder Church.

Zwischen Barock und Rokoko

Eine Kirche, leichtfüßig und beschwingt wie ein Gartenpalais – das scheint dem Prunner-Schüler Matthias Krinner vorgeschwebt zu sein, als er der altehrwürdigen Linzer *Minoritenkirche* ihre neue Form gab. Heute ist die Kirche in die Nordfassade des Landhauses integriert. In der Reformationszeit bemühten sich die Stände vergeblich, daraus ein protestantisches Gotteshaus zu machen. Nun dient sie unter anderem als „Landhauskirche". Beliebt bei den Linzern sind die feierlichen Gottesdienste, die von den Seitenaltargemälden des Kremser Schmidt und dem Hochaltarblatt von Bartolomeo Altomonte festlich umrahmt werden.

Bei den sieben Engelsfürsten

Wer das Innere der *Ursulinenkirche* betritt, die mit ihren beiden wuchtigen Zwiebeltürmen die Landstraße überragt, dem fällt zunächst einmal das prachtvolle Hochaltarbild ins Auge. Es stammt von Martin Altomonte, der es noch im Alter von 80 Jahren gemalt hat. Das Hauptbild ist den „sieben Engelsfürsten" gewidmet. Zahlreiche prunkvolle Seitenaltäre verstärken die opulente Wirkung dieses spätbarocken Bauwerks.

Between Baroque and Rococo

A church as light and airy as a garden palace seems to have been uppermost in the mind of Matthias Krinner, a pupil of Prunner, when he gave Linz' venerable Minorite Church *its present Form. Today, the church is integrated with the north facade of the Assembly House. During the Reformation, the estates of the realm tried unsuccessfully to have it converted to a protestant church. Today, it is known as the "Assembly House Church" and is especially popular with the people in Linz for its festive services framed by side altar paintings by Kremser Schmidt and the High Altar work by Bartolomeo Altomonte.*

The Seven Angelic Princes

The most striking thing a visitor notices when entering the Church of the Ursulines *which dominates Landstrasse with its imposing onion domes, is the magnificent altar painting. It is the work of Martin Altomonte who finished work on it at the age of 80. The main painting is dedicated to the "seven angelic princes". Numerous splendid side altars underline the opulent impression of this late baroque church.*

Obst gab's an der Klosterpforte

Als die Karmeliter nach fast vierzigjähriger Bauzeit die erste Messe in der von Johann Michael Prunner erbauten und von Diego Francesco Carlone mit Stuckarbeiten ausgeführten Kirche feiern konnten, verfügte Linz nicht nur über eine prunkvolle Barockkirche mehr, sondern auch über eine bei der Bevölkerung besonders beliebte Attraktion: Hinter dem Kloster befand sich nämlich ein über 10.000 m² großer Klostergarten, dessen Obst- und Gemüseproduktion auch an der Klosterpforte zum Verkauf gelangte. Heute ist die *Karmeliterkirche* freilich längst vom Stadtkern umschlossen, in dem sie mit ihrer eigenwilligen Fassade eine besonders dominante Stellung einnimmt.

Von Altar zu Altar

Linz verfügte – im Verhältnis zu seiner Größe – schon immer über eine Vielzahl von Kirchen und Kapellen. Viele dieser architektonisch meist besonders kostbaren Kleinodien sind auch heute noch erhalten. Da ist zum Beispiel die berühmte *Seminarkirche* in der Harrachstraße, deren Pläne kein Geringerer als der Wiener Belvedere-Erbauer Lukas von Hildebrandt gezeichnet hat, nach welchen Johann Michael Prunner die Bauausführung übernahm. Von Prunner selbst stammt die kleine, aber besonders schmuckreiche *Kirche der Barmherzigen Brüder*, ein geschwungener Zentralbau mit einem Hochaltarbild des Kremser Schmidt, einer Immaculata-Darstellung, die zu den Hauptwerken des Künstlers zählt. Die Kapuzinerkirche beherbergt einen Gedenkstein, der an den Tod des Türkenbezwingers Graf Montecuccoli erinnert, der in Linz im Jahre 1680 verstarb. Vom Linzer Baumeister Matthias Krinner wurde das *Elisabethinenkloster*, von Paul Ulrich Trientl die *Elisabethinenkirche* geschaffen, die bereits frühklassizistische Züge aufweist. Der jenseits der Donau gelegene Stadtteil Urfahr verfügt mit der *Pfarrkirche hl. Josef* ebenfalls über eine barocke Saalkirche. Und moderne Kirchenbauten wie *St. Michael* (Am Bindermichl), *St. Konrad* (Froschberg) und *St. Theresia* (Keferfeld) zeugen von einer Fortführung der alten Linzer Tradition des kunstvollen Sakralbaus.

Fruit at the Gate of the Monastery

After forty years of construction, the Carmelites finally celebrated the first mass in their new church built by Johann Michael Prunner and with stucco work by Diego Francesco Carlone. Linz was not only richer by yet another magnificent baroque church, but had also gained another popular attraction: behind the building was a 10,000 m² fruit plantation and vegetable garden; its produce was sold in front of the church. Today, the Church of Carmelites *has long since been surrounded by the city centre, but its striking facade still dominates the surroundings.*

From Altar to Altar

Linz has always, in relation to its size, boasted an extremely large number of churches and chapels. Many of these architectural gems can still be seen and enjoyed today. The Seminar Church, *for example, in Harrachstrasse, the plans for which were completed by none other than the builder of Vienna's Belvedere, Lukas von Hildebrandt, was later to be constructed by Johann Michael Prunner. Prunner himself was solely responsible for the small but particularly decorative* Kirche der Barmherzigen Brüder *(Church of the Merciful Brothers), with its lively architectural line and an altar painting by Kremser Schmidt. It is an Immaculata portrayal and numbers among the artist's finest works. The Capuchine Church contains a memorial plaque in honour of Count Montecuccoli, victor in battles against the Turks, who died in Linz in 1680. The Linz master builder Matthias Krinner was responsible for the* Elizabethine Convent, *and Paul Ulrich Trientl for the* Elizabethine Church, *with its early classicist touches. Just across the Danube in an area known as Urfahr, the* Parish Church of St. Joseph *is another example of high baroque. The old tradition of sacral architecture has been continued to the present day as witnessed by such modern churches as* St. Michael *(Am Bindemichl),* St. Konrad *(Froschberg) and* St. Theresia *(Keferfeld).*

Gegenüberliegende Seite: Seminarkirche mit Priesterseminar.
Opposite page: Seminar Church with Priests' Seminar.

BÜRGERLICHES LINZ
Bourgeois Linz

Der Hauptplatz an der Einmündung der Klosterstraße.
Main Square at the beginning of Klosterstrasse.

Ein Geschichtsbuch, 219 x 60 m

Er sieht aus wie ein Saal unter offenem Himmel.
Der Linzer *Hauptplatz* ist weitläufig wie ein
Getreidefeld und intim wie ein schöner alter Hof
zugleich. Trotz seiner Größe von 13.140 m² wirkt
der Platz niemals unpersönlich und ist heute wie
vor sechshundert Jahren kommunikativ, einla-
dend und gleichzeitig repräsentativ.

Seine heutigen Ausmaße erhielt er im 13. Jahrhundert. Und es war für die Linzer Bevölkerung
damals schon ein gewagtes Stück, einen Platz
von derartigen Dimensionen in den Stadtkern
einzuplanen. Schließlich mußten deshalb Stadt-
mauern erweitert und Befestigungsanlagen ausgebaut werden; die gesamte Struktur des alten
Linz wurde von Grund auf verändert. Daß das
alles eine Menge Geld kostete, liegt auf der
Hand. Linz hatte sich dazumal indessen bereits
als blühende Handelsstadt etabliert. Die Grund-
stückspreise waren hier so hoch wie nirgendwo
anders. Jeder bessere Kaufmann wollte wenig-
stens eine Nische des Platzes sein eigen nennen.
So ist es übrigens auch erklärbar, daß der Hauptplatz von besonders vielen kleinen Häusern mit

A History Book, 219 x 60 Metres

*It looks like an open air Great Hall. The Main
Square of Linz, Hauptplatz, is as vast as a field of
grain and as intimate as a beautiful old courtyard. Despite its size of 13,140 m², the square is
never impersonal and is as communicative, invit-
ing and at the same time just as grand as it was
600 years ago.*

*Its present dimensions were laid down in the 13th
century and this reveals a great deal of boldness
on the part of the residents of Linz in those days:
they opted for a square of extraordinary size in
relation to the extent of town. Not only that city
walls had to be extended and new defences plan-
ned; the entire structure of old Linz was irrevocab-
ly altered. Obviously, it all cost quite a lot of mon-
ey. Linz was already a thriving centre of trade.
Property rates were higher here than anywhere
else, and so of course every merchant worth his
salt was keen to call at least a tiny niche of the
square his own. This is the reason that the square
is surrounded by so many small houses with narrow facades, most of which, however, extend far
back in compensation. The merchants of those*

schmalen Fassaden gesäumt wird, die ihre mangelnde Breite indessen durch eine überdurchschnittliche Tiefe wieder ausgleichen. Schließlich benötigten gerade die damaligen Kaufleute viel Lagerraum und Magazine.

Durch seine Größe eignete sich der Platz seit jeher für Massenveranstaltungen aller Art. Als Erzherzog Ferdinand am 26. Mai 1521 Anna von Ungarn heiratete, wurde vor einer vielköpfigen Zuschauermenge das berühmte „Losensteiner Turnier" ausgetragen. Später rollten auf dem Hauptplatz die Köpfe. Hier wurden die Rädelsführer der Bauernkriege gleichsam als Massenspektakel öffentlich hingerichtet. Bis zum Jahr 1716 wurden alle möglichen Übeltäter am Pranger dem Gespött der Menge preisgegeben.

Wo einst der Pranger stand, erhebt sich heute das Wahrzeichen von Linz schlechthin: die 1723 vom Steinmetz Sebastian Stumpfegger nach einem Entwurf von Antonio Beduzzi ausgeführte *Dreifaltigkeitssäule*. Dreifach ist hier nicht nur die göttliche Einheit, sondern auch der Anlaß, der zu

days needed space at the back for storage and wares.

Its size makes the square ideal for large assemblies. When Archduke Ferdinand married Anna of Hungary on May 26th, 1521, the famous "Losenstein Tournament" took place here before a teeming throng. Later, heads were to roll on the same square. The leaders of the peasant uprising were executed here in the form of a public spectacle. Until the year 1716 all manner of misdemeanors were punished here on the square's pillory, fair game for the mockery of passers-by.

Where the pillory once stood is now the site of one of Linz' most typical landmarks, a Column of the Holy Trinity, *completed in 1732 by sculptor Sebastian Stumpfegger after a design by Antonio Beduzzi. The number "three" figures not only in the allegory of divine unity but also in the lifting of the plague in 1713.*

While this impressive column marks the centre of the square, the Rathaus, *or City Hall, symbolizes the gradual rise of the middle class. The gothic*

Linzer Hauptplatz. Detail vom Brunnen.
Main Square of Linz. Detail of the fountain.

Linzer Hauptplatz. Detail der Dreifaltigkeitssäule.
Main Square of Linz. Detail of the Holy Trinity Column.

Hauptplatz. Detail vom Brunnen. – Main Square. Detail of the fountain.

Gegenüberliegende Seite: Barocke Fassaden am Hauptplatz mit dem Linzer Schloß im Hintergrund.
Opposite page: Baroque facades on the Main Square with the Castle of Linz in the background.

Dreifaltigkeitssäule auf dem Hauptplatz. – Holy Trinity Column on the Main Square.

diesem Bau führte. Die Säule wurde zum Dank für die 1704 überstandene Kriegsgefahr, die 1712 in Schranken gewiesene Feuersbrunst und das Ende der Pest 1713 errichtet.

Während die Dreifaltigkeitssäule das Zentrum des Platzes markiert, ist das alte *Rathaus* jenes des aufstrebenden Linzer Bürgertums. Der gotische Bau wurde 1513 errichtet und später mehrmals umgestaltet.

Was für das Rathaus gilt, stimmt übrigens auch für die meisten Häuser des Hauptplatzes: Sie sind durchwegs wesentlich älter, als sie auf den ersten Blick scheinen. Die vielen Linzer Stadtbrände auf der einen und der sich stetig wandelnde Geschmack auf der anderen Seite haben dafür gesorgt, daß der ursprüngliche gotische Baukern des Platzes sich immer wieder ein neues äußeres Kleid zulegte.

Völlig verändert wurde gegenüber früheren Zeiten der sogenannte *Brückenkopf*, an dem sich der Hauptplatz zur *Nibelungenbrücke* über die Donau hin verjüngt. Die beiden Gebäude wurden erst 1947 fertiggestellt.

Fast jedes Haus am Linzer Hauptplatz weiß irgendeine Geschichte zu erzählen. Da gibt es etwa das am Hauptplatz Nr. 18 gelegene *Feichtingerhaus,* das durch ein hübsches Glockenspiel mit Bruckner-Themen auffällt. Und im Haus Hauptplatz *Nr. 27* fand der berüchtigte französische Polizeiminister Joseph Fouché in den Jahren 1818–1820 Unterschlupf im Exil.

Der Hauptplatz ist heute Schauplatz vieler Märkte, vom idyllischen Weihnachts- über den quicklebendigen Floh- bis zu einem kleinen Obst- und Gemüsemarkt.

building was finished in 1513 and was subsequently rebuilt.

The architectural evolution of the City Hall also holds true of many buildings around the Main Square, most of them are considerably older than they at first appear to be. The long series of fires which has plagued the history of Linz as well as constantly changing architectural taste are responsible for the changes – the medieval foundation have taken on many a new dress in the course of centuries.

On the Main Square looking towards the Danube we come to the Brückenkopf (Bridgehead) and Nibelungenbrücke (Bridge of the Nibelungs), buildings which look entirely different from their namesakes, both were reconstructed in 1947.

Nearly every house on the square has its own story to tell. At Nr. 18, for example, the Feichtingerhaus has its own "Glockenspiel" which plays themes by Bruckner. In the house of Nr. 27, the infamous French Minister of Police Joseph Fouché took up residence-in-exile from 1818 to 1820.

Today the Main Square forms the backdrop for many different kinds of markets, from the idyllic Christmas Fair to the lively and colorful fleamarket as well as stands for fruits and vegetables.

Haus Hauptplatz 21. Fenster-Relief „Wilde Männer". – House no. 21 on the Main Square with the relief "The Wild Men".

Gegenüberliegende Seite: Der achteckige Eckerker des alten Rathauses.
Opposite page: The octogonal bay-window of the Old City Hall.

A Town Along the Road

Linz is often jokingly referred to that way. And indeed, Linz did not grow outwards, star-shaped from the centre, like many other large cities. Even in the city centre you can detect a trace of its former village character.

Landstrasse begins at Taubenmarkt (Pigeon Market), *a graceful little square between Promenade and Graben, with its old name recalling the animal market which used to be here. Today, it is the centre of the thriving shopping area and where once fields and suburbs lined a country road, large department stores, exclusive shops and shopping arcades vie for custom.*

Continuing from Taubenmarkt, one of the most beautiful secular buildings of Linz can be seen on the immediate right, Palais Weissenwolf. *The work of Johann Michael Prunner set new architectural standards in what was once merely a suburb.*

At the corner of the street called Spittelwiese, it is worth pausing at a house named Florianer Stifts-

Das Palais des Kaufmännischen Vereins.
The palace of the mercantile association.
Unten: Das Starhembergische Freihaus und der Eingang zum City-Einkaufszentrum „Arkade".
Below: The Starhemberg House and the entrance to the City-shopping centre "Arkade".

Linz an der Landstraße

So wird die Stadt immer wieder scherzhaft genannt. Und in der Tat ist Linz nicht, wie viele andere große Städte, sternförmig um ein Zentrum angelegt. In der Stadtanlage schimmert noch heute eine dörfliche Vergangenheit durch. Die Landstraße beginnt am *Taubenmarkt,* einem überschaubaren kleinen Platz zwischen Promenade und Graben, der seinen Namen dem Kleintiermarkt verdankt, der in früherer Zeit hier abgehalten wurde. Man befindet sich im Herzen der Einkaufsstadt Linz, und wo früher Felder und kleine Vorstadtsiedlungen die Landstraße säumten, da findet man heute Großkaufhäuser, gediegene kleine Geschäfte und Einkaufsarkaden. Wenn man vom Taubenmarkt kommt, so befindet sich gleich rechter Hand einer der schönsten barocken Profanbauten des alten Linz: Im *Palais Weissenwolf* setzte Johann Michael Prunner neue architektonische Maßstäbe in der damaligen Vorstadt.

Ecke Spittelwiese lohnt sich ein Abstecher in

Gegenüberliegende Seite: Oben: Blick vom Brückenkopf zum „Alten Dom".
Opposite page: Above: View from the Brückenkopf to the "Old Cathedral".
Unten: Treiben auf dem Flohmarkt.
Below: The hustle and bustle of the fleamarket.

Der „Klosterhof" mit dem schönsten Biergarten von Linz.
The "Klosterhof" with the most beautiful beer garden of Linz.

Die geschäftige Landstraße mit dem Taubenmarkt im Hintergrund.
The busy Landstrasse with Taubenmarkt in the background.

den Hof des alten *Florianer Stiftshauses* (Landstraße 22), dessen Arkaden ein schönes Beispiel sind, wie man in Linz zur Zeit der Renaissance gebaut hat. Das alte *Baumgartenberger Stiftshaus* ist heute besser als *Klosterhof* bekannt und wird von den Linzern vor allem wegen des von zahlreichen Kastanienbäumen überschatteten Biergartens geliebt. Wem Stuck und Marmor mehr zusagen als Hopfen und Gerste, kommt hier allerdings ebenfalls auf seine Rechnung: Der Renaissancebau ist nicht nur durch seine schönen Stiegenaufgänge und die Aula im ersten Stock von Bedeutung, sondern auch durch eine Pietà aus dem Jahre 1420, eine Immaculata im Stiegenhaus und einen geschnitzten hl. Florian an der Außenfassade, der hier freilich wohl in erster Linie als Durstlösch-Patron zu bezeichnen ist.

Am Haus *Landstraße 36* erinnert eine Gedenktafel an ein historisches Ereignis aus der nahen Vergangenheit: Im ehemaligen „Hotel Schiff", dem heutigen Zentralkino, fielen am 12. Fe-

haus *(Landstrasse Nr. 22) and having a look at the arcades, a fine example of Renaissance architecture. The old* Baumgartner Stiftshaus *is better known today as the* Klosterhof *and is popular with locals thanks in particular to its shady beer garden with its wealth of old chestnut trees. If stucco work and marble mean more to you than hops and barley, this building is also worth visiting. It dates from the Renaissance and boasts splendid staircases, a Great Hall on the first floor, a Pietà from 1420, an immaculata in the staircase and, finally, a carved St. Florian on the facade. It may be said of him that he not only douses fires but also quenches thirst.*

A commemorative plaque on the house at Landstrasse 36 *reminds us of a historical event of recent times: In the former "Hotel Schiff" – today the Central Cinema – the first shots of February 12th, 1934 were fired, ushering in the February riots. Just over a crossing named Mozartkreuzung is the protestant Martin Luther Church. It is easy to overlook this building for the simple reason*

Stimmungsvolle Beisl-Szene in der Linzer Altstadt. – The atmospheric taverns in the Old Town of Linz.
Gegenüberliegende Seite: Beeindruckend präsentiert sich das im Renaissancestil erbaute Nordportal des Landhauses im nächtlichen
Altstadtensemble. – Opposite page: An impressive view of the neo-Renaissance North Portal of the Provincial Assembly at night.

Detail der Dreifaltigkeitssäule. – Detail of the Holy Trinity Column.

Allabendlich verwandelt sich die Altstadt in ein Mekka für Nachtschwärmer.
The Old Town becomes a mecca for night-owls every evening.

45

bruar 1934 jene Schüsse, die zu den Februarunruhen im damaligen Ständestaat führten. Wenn man die *Mozartkreuzung* überquert, erreicht man nach einigen Schritten die evangelische *Martin-Luther-Kirche.* Daß man sie nicht gleich auf den ersten Blick sieht, hat seinen Grund im Toleranzpatent Josefs II. Dort wurde nämlich festgelegt, daß protestantische Gotteshäuser stets einen „Respektabstand" von mindestens 50 Metern zur Straße aufzuweisen hätten. Einen solchen Abstand hatte das Linzer *Kaufmännische Vereinshaus* an der Ecke zur Bismarckstraße nicht nötig. Es ist ein Glanzstück bürgerlichen Selbstbewußtseins. 1611 als „Herrenhaus" erbaut, dient es bis heute mit seinem prunkvollen Spiegelsaal für Ball- und Konzertveranstaltungen.

that in the Writ of Tolerance issued by Josef II protestant churches had to observe a "respectful distance" of 50 metres from the street.
No such distance had to be observed by the Kaufmännische Vereinshaus, *a mercantile house at the corner of Bismarckstrasse. It is a brilliant example of the self-confidence and pride of the local bourgeoisie. Built as a townhouse in 1611, today its glittering Hall of Mirrors is the site of balls and concerts.*

Die neugestaltete Weihnachtsbeleuchtung entlang der Landstraße.
The new Christmas lighting on Landstrasse.
Gegenüberliegende Seite: Weitläufig und trotzdem intim wie ein schöner alter Hof – der nächtliche Hauptplatz.
Opposite page: Vast but still as intimate as an old courtyard – the Main Square at night.

Vom Reichengäßchen zum Armenhaus: Ein Altstadtbummel

Am *Hofberg,* der von der Donau hinauf steil zum Schloß ansteigt, wandelt man auf den Spuren des Mittelalters. Der Fährtensucher, der an den Häusern *Hofberg Nr. 6* und *Nr. 8* vorbeikommt, tut jedenfalls gut daran, dort eine Zeitlang zu verweilen. Zunächst wird er nur ein versperrtes Gitter vorfinden, das in eine finstere Häuserschlucht mündet. Bei näherem Hinsehen wird er jedoch merken, daß er sich hier am Eingang zum *Reichengäßchen,* einem der ältesten Teile von Linz, befindet. Es wurde erst 1957 freigelegt und ist nur etwa 50 m lang. Bei diesem Gäßchen handelt es sich um eine sogenannte „Reiche": So nannte man im Mittelalter jene hinterhofartigen Anlagen, die für Löscharbeiten, als Regenwasserabfluß und auch als Abtritt dienten.

Die Linzer Altstadt ist voll von solchen Kuriositäten und bemerkenswerten Gebäuden. Bleiben wir gleich am Hofberg. Da gibt es unter der *Nr. 4* ein Renaissancehaus aus dem Jahre 1578, in dem Kaiser Josef II. 1783 und 1786 genächtigt hat. Das Haus *Nr. 2* nahm einst ebenfalls einen prominenten Gast auf: Im „Hotel Krebs" wohnte im Jahre 1902 der Winnetou-Erfinder Karl May. Ihn verband eine enge Freundschaft mit jenem Linzer Photographen, der auch die berühmten Photos von Karl May in Old Shatterhand- und Kara-Ben-Nemsi-Pose geschaffen hat.

Das *Kremsmünsterer Stiftshaus* (Altstadt Nr. 10) wurde zwischen 1578 und 1580 vom Landhaus-Architekten Christoph Canevale auf den Grundfesten eines noch älteren Gebäudes errichtet, in

From the Lane of the Rich to the Poor House: A Stroll Through the Old Town

The Hofberg, *a hill which rises steeply up from the Danube and whose paths lead up to the Castle, offers a chance to catch a glimpse of the Middle Ages. Don't rush past the houses at Hofberg Nr. 6 and Nr. 8, but pause a while. First you will notice a closed lattice gate, which leads to a dark alley. Closer inspection, however, reveals the entrance to the* Lane of the Rich, *the oldest section of Linz. It was not reopened until 1957 and is only 50 metres long. The name of this lane refers to a "Reiche", which in the Middle Ages was an expression for alleys which served for the purpose of fire fighting, rain water drainage and waste disposal.*

The Old Town is full of such curiosities and remarkable buildings. Let's stay a moment on Hofberg. At Nr. 4 there is a Renaissance house from the year 1578 in which Emperor Josef II stayed over night in 1783 and 1786. The house at Nr. 2 also hosted an important guest: under the name of "Hotel Krebs" it housed the famous German writer of westerns, Karl May. He spent some time here in 1902 visiting a local photographer who was known for his photos of the successful author in the garb of his fictional heroes.

The Kremsmünsterer Stiftshaus (Altstadt Nr. 10) *was built by the architect of the Assembly House, Christoph Canevale, between 1578 and 1580 on the foundations of a much older building which is the traditional site of the death of Emperor Friedrich III. A gourmet restaurant has recently been established in the newly restored gabled house. At Altstadt Nr. 12 is another house with connec-*

Blick durch die Badgasse zum Hofberg. – View of Hofberg from Badgasse.

Kremsmünsterer Stiftshof. Portal mit Abtwappen. – Courtyard of the Kremsmünster. Portal with the coat of arms of the abbots.

Runderker am Haus Ecke Hofgasse/Hofberg.
Round bay-window of a house at the corner of Hofgasse/Hofberg.

Pittoreske Hausfassaden auf dem Römerberg. – Picturesque house facades on Römerberg.

Barockportal am Hofberg. – Baroque portal on Hofberg.

dem Kaiser Friedrich III. gestorben sein soll. In dem erst unlängst vollständig renovierten Erkerhaus befindet sich neuerdings auch ein Feinschmeckerrestaurant.

Auch die Hausnummer Altstadt Nr. 12 hat indirekt etwas mit Essen und Trinken zu tun: Hier stand früher die Stadtwaage, die dem Gebäude auch seinen Namen, *Waaghaus*, gab. Schon 1590 wurde das Haus jedoch auch als Schulgebäude adaptiert, in dem die Stadtpfarrschule untergebracht war, die im Volksmund auch „Waagschule" hieß.

Auch Wolfgang Amadeus Mozart hat seinen Namen in die Waagschale geworfen, als er den Linzern eine eigene Symphonie widmete. Komponiert hat er sie im *Starhembergischen Freihaus* (Altstadt Nr. 17), wo das damals schon gar nicht mehr kindliche „Wunderkind" aus Salzburg im November des Jahres 1783 logierte. Es war übrigens nicht das einzige Mal, daß Mozart Linz aufsuchte. 1785 kam er wieder und stieg diesmal im Gasthaus *Zum schwarzen Bock* (Altstadt Nr. 22) ab, in dem – nebenbei bemerkt – die große Burg-Mimin Hedwig Bleibtreu 1868 das Licht der Welt erblickte. Der alte Einkehrgasthof wurde im Bombenhagel des Zweiten Weltkriegs zerstört und 1957 nach alten Plänen wieder aufgebaut.

Und wenn wir unseren Altstadtbummel in einem „Reichengäßchen" begonnen haben, so ist es nur recht und billig, wenn wir ihn in einem Armenhaus beenden. Diese Funktion hatte nämlich das vom Linzer Bürgermeister Johann Adam Pruner 1737 errichtete und nach ihm benannte *Prunerstift* (Fabrikstraße Nr. 10) vor allem zu erfüllen. Hier befindet sich eine schöne Barockkapelle. Das einstige Waisenheim und spätere Armenhaus ist identisch mit der dazumal allseits beliebten „Rumford'schen Suppenanstalt". Heute ist im vorbildlich renovierten Prunerstift die Musikschule der Stadt Linz untergebracht.

tions to eating and drinking, if only indirectly. This was the site of the City Scales and the name of the house is indeed Waaghaus, *or House of the Scales. By 1590, however, it had already been adapted as a school building in which the parish school was housed – locals called it the "Scales School".*

Wolfgang Amadeus Mozart is another famous name to be weighed in the scales of Linz, for he dedicated an entire symphony to the people of the city. He composed it in the Starhembergischen Freihaus *(Altstadt Nr. 17) where the "Wunderkind", who was not actually so childish any more, lived in 1783. This was not the only time that Mozart visited Linz. He came in 1785 again, this time staying in an inn called* Zum schwarzen Bock – The Black Ram – *(Altstadt Nr. 22) where, by the way, the great actor Hedwig Bleibtreu was born in 1986. The old inn was destroyed by bombs during the Second World War but was rebuilt according to old plans in 1957.*

And as we began our stroll in the "Lane of the Rich" it seems more than appropriate to conclude it at a Poor House. Here is the Prunerstift *(Fabrikstraße 10), erected by the burgomaster of Linz, Johann Adam Pruner, in 1737 and named after him. The baroque chapel is of considerable interest. This former orphanage and later poor house was mentioned as the "Rumford'sche Suppenanstalt" or "Rumford Soup Kitchen". Today it is beautifully renovated and houses the music school of the City of Linz.*

KULTURELLES LINZ
Cultural Linz

Zeitkultur am Hafen präsentiert der Posthof, ein Festspielhaus der Gegenkultur.
Avant-garde at the harbour in Posthof, a festival hall for new culture.
Gegenüberliegende Seite: Das multifunktionelle Design Center ist eine Komposition technischer Ästhetik.
Opposite page: The multi-functional Design Center is a composition of aesthetic technology.

Rave-Fest im Linzer Posthof. – Rave Party in the Linz Posthof.

Harmonisch fügt sich die VOEST-Brücke in die Donaulandschaft. – The VOEST bridge blends in with the landscape.

Konstantin Wecker beim „Linz-Fest". – Konstantin Wecker at the "Linz Festival".

Das Design Center:
Linz auf dem Weg ins dritte Jahrtausend
Der multifunktionale Komplex, 1993 eröffnet, ist
eine Komposition technischer Ästhetik. Die fast
14.000 Quadratmeter große Dachhaut besteht
aus einer Stahlkonstruktion mit Glaspaneelen.
Auf diese Weise bietet das *Design Center* den fas-
zinierenden Effekt eines Tageslichthauses. Ein
ausgeklügeltes System gibt die Möglichkeit,
schnellstens notwendige Adaptierungen für
unterschiedliche Veranstaltungsformen vorneh-
men zu können.
Das Design Center ist somit ein idealer Ort für
Messen, Produktpräsentationen, Kongresse,
Bankette und Tagungen sowie Ausstellungen von
internationalem Format.

The Design Centre:
Linz on the Way to the Third Millenium
This multi-functional complex, which opened at
the end of 1993, is an aesthetically pleasing
technical composition. The roofing skin consists
of a steel construction with glass panels and is
almost 14,000 square metres. It gives the Design
Center *the fascinating effect of a daylight*
building. An ingenious system allows for the
possibility of making all the necessary alterations
for staging a variety of events.
The Design Centre is thus an ideal place for
trade fairs, product presentations, congresses,
banquets and conferences, as well as international
exhibitions.

Der Posthof:
Zeitkultur am Hafen

Der *Posthof* war früher tatsächlich einmal ein Posthof. Zu den Zeiten, als es in der Stadt durch allzu natürliche Umweltverschmutzung bestialisch roch, wurden in den Hallen Pferde gewechselt. Das vor sich hindämmernde Gebäude wurde in den frühen achtziger Jahren von jungen Linzer Künstlern entdeckt. Die „Rockhaus"-Bewegung entstand und erhielt früher als ähnliche Initiativen in anderen Städten ein offenes Ohr bei den Stadtvätern.

Seit 1985 gibt es nun dieses „Festspielhaus der Gegenkultur", das heute Posthof 1 heißt. Während der Besucherstrom von Jahr zu Jahr anwuchs, kamen die Planungen für einen Erweiterungsbau in ein konkretes Stadium.

Seit 1990 gibt es den Posthof 2. Im größten zeitgenössischen Kulturkomplex Österreichs wird eine überaus bunte Palette geboten – vom Theater über Musik, Kabarett und Kleinkunst bis zu einer Produktionsstätte für nationale und internationale Künstler und für regionale Initiativen.

The Posthof:
Contemporary Culture on the Waterfront

As its name indicates, the Posthof *was at one time a post house. In the days when the streets still stank as a result of all-too-natural environmental pollution, horses used to be changed in these halls. In the early 1980s some young artists discovered the building still in a kind of twilight state. That was the start of the "Rockhaus" movement, which received support from the city elders of Linz earlier than was the case with similar initiatives in other cities.*

This "festival hall of the alternative culture", today called Posthof 1, was founded in 1985. Since then, the number of visitors has steadily increased from year to year and the plans for an extension have taken concrete form.

Since 1990 a Posthof 2 has also come into being. The largest complex for contemporary culture in Austria, the Posthof, presents a wide range of events – from theatre to music, from cabaret to productions by Austrian and international artists as well as regional projects.

Begeistertes Publikum beim „Linz-Fest". – Delighted audience at the "Linz Festival".

Darbietungen des bunten Kleinkunstvolkes beim beliebten „Pflasterspektakel".
Creators of arts and crafts at the popular "Sidewalk Spectacle".

„Pflasterspektakel" in der City: Eine Arena der guten Laune

Seit vielen Jahren verwandeln Künstler an drei Tagen im Juli die Landstraße und den Hauptplatz zu einem südländisch anmutenden Straßenfest. Dort tummeln sich Straßenmusiker, Clowns, Fakire, Gaukler, Pantomime- und Zauberkünstler, Maler, Märchenerzähler, kurz Menschen, die ihre Zuhörer und Zuseher auf eigentlich archaische Weise unterhalten. Bei Schönwetter strömen längst mehr als 200.000 Besucher zu dem *Pflasterspektakel* in die Innenstadt, um die Darbietungen dieses bunten Kleinkunstvolkes zu genießen.

The Street Spectacle in the City Centre: A Forum for Good Vibes

For many years now, three days in July have seen the Landstrasse and the Main Square transformed by artists into a street festival reminiscent of those found in southern cultures. There are street musicians, clowns, fakirs, jugglers, mimes and conjurors, artists, storytellers – in short, people who entertain their audience in a way which has actually become archaic today.
If the weather is good, well over 200,000 visitors pour into the city centre to the Street Spectacle *to enjoy what these colourful performers have to offer.*

Das Brucknerhaus:
Eine Weihestätte für den Genius loci

Für kein Gebäude seit dem Maria-Empfängnis-Dom haben die Linzer so lange und ausdauernd gesammelt wie für das *Brucknerhaus*. 1969 war es dann soweit: Der Grundstein für eines der modernsten Konzerthäuser der Welt konnte gelegt werden. Als Architekt hatte man den Finnen Heikki Siren beauftragt, der einen ebenso sachlichen wie eindrucksvollen Rundbau an der

The Bruckner House:
Dedicated to the Genius loci

Not since the building of the Maria-Empfängnis-Dom, or New Cathedral, have the people of Linz collected donations for so long and with such assiduity as for the Bruckner House. *In 1969 the time had come – the cornerstone for one of the most modern concert houses in the world was laid. The architect was Heikki Siren, a Finn, who conceived a simple but impressive round building near the*

Donaulände geschaffen hat. Die Akustik des bis zu 1.400 Menschen fassenden großen Saals ist kristallklar und frei von jedem Nachhall. Der 103 m lange Wandelgang hinter einer wuchtigen geschwungenen Glasfront gibt den Blick auf den Pöstlingberg und das Hügelland des Mühlviertels frei. Das Haus läßt sich spielend in ein Konferenzzentrum oder einen Ballsaal verwandeln. Beim Eröffnungskonzert im Jahre 1974 mit Herbert von Karajan und den Wiener Philharmonikern stand selbstverständlich ein Meisterwerk des Genius loci auf dem Programm: die 7. Symphonie von Anton Bruckner. Er sollte auch weiterhin der musikalische Schutzgeist des Hauses bleiben: Ihm zu Ehren wird jeden Herbst das „Internationale Brucknerfest" mit Dirigenten und Orchestern von Weltrang veranstaltet.

Um zur klassischen „Hochkultur" einen modernen Kontrapunkt zu setzen, ist im Brucknerhaus jedoch dank der „Ars Electronica", einer in ihrer Art weltweit singulären Veranstaltung, auch die Moderne zu Hause. Zu einem fixen Bestandteil des Linzer Kulturlebens sind auch die berühmten „Klangwolken" geworden, die im Donaupark vor dem Brucknerhaus akustische sowie optische Musik- und Raumerlebnisse höchst ungewöhnlicher Prägung ermöglichen.

Danube. The acoustics of the Great Hall, which seats up to 1,444 people, are crystal clear and free of even the slightest echo. A promenade area with a length of 103 metres reveals a view of the Pöstlingberg and the hilly terrain of the vicinity known as Mühlviertel through the monumental curved glass walls. The house can be easily adapted as a conference centre or a ballroom. At the festive opening in 1974, the Vienna Philharmonic under Herbert von Karajan included a work of the Genius loci on the programme, the 7th Symphony of Anton Bruckner. In fact, Bruckner was to remain the guiding spirit of the house and in his honour, the "International Bruckner Festival" is organized each autumn in which conductors and orchestras from all over the world take part.
In order to provide a certain counterpoint to classical culture in the traditional sense, the "Ars Electronica" takes place annually in the Bruckner House and has developed into a contemporary festival unique in Europe. Another regular feature of the cultural scenery in Linz are the "Sound Clouds" which are organized regularly in the Danube Park in front of the Bruckner House. These events are multi-media presentations in which sound, music and spectacle combine to form an extraordinary multi-media experience.

Ars Electronica 1980 – „Blue Star" von Otto Piene. – Ars Electronica 1980 – "Blue Star" of Otto Piene.

Das Landestheater mit der Promenade. – The Landestheater with the promenade.
Gegenüberliegende Seite: „Carmina Burana" im Landestheater. – Opposite page: "Carmina Burana" in the Provincial Theatre.

Vom Ballhaus zum Landestheater
1732 wurde ein alter Stadel an der Donau zu einem Schauspielhaus umfunktioniert, einem „Komödiantenstadl" gewissermaßen. Einige Jahrzehnte später wurde daraus das städtische „Wassertheater", das allerdings bald im Lauf eines Hochwassers von den Donauwellen hinweggespült wurde. Das Theater übersiedelte also in das schon 1695 von Carlo Antonio Carlone errichtete Ballhaus, dessen Redoutensaal zu einer veritablen Guckkastenbühne ausgebaut wurde. 1802 wurde daraus ein landesstädtisches Theater mit jener klassizistischen Empire-Fassade, die dem *Landestheater* auch heute noch sein charakteristisches Aussehen verleiht.

From Medieval Ballroom to Regional Theatre
In 1732 an old barn on the Danube was turned into a theatre, a sort of "actors' playhouse". Several decades later it became the municipal "Wassertheater" although this was soon washed away by the waves of the Danube during a flood. The theatre then moved to a ballroom house built by Carlo Antonio Carlone, whose main ballroom was extended into a veritable picture-frame stage. In 1802 this became a provincial theatre and received the classicistic imperial facade which gives the Landestheater *its characteristic appearance even today.*

Kapelle im Garten des Landeskulturzentrums. – Chapel in the garden of the Provincial Culture Centre.

Ein Kulturzentrum für alle

Bildung ist bei den Ursulinen an der Landstraße schon seit 1680 vermittelt worden. Seit der Orden 1968 ausgezogen ist, stehen hier abermals Bildung und Kultur auf dem Programm, wenn diese auch keineswegs in schulmeisterlicher Weise angeboten werden. In den siebziger Jahren wurde der 1692–1697 von Georg und Franz Pruckmayr geschaffene Barockbau gänzlich renoviert und vom Land Oberösterreich als *Kulturzentrum Ursulinenhof* der Öffentlichkeit übergeben. Es gibt genug Raum für das blühende Kunstleben Oberösterreichs. Und der „Theaterkeller" wurde dem Landestheater als Experimentierbühne zur Verfügung gestellt.

Ein Stift für nordische Zöglinge

Als solches diente das ehemalige „Collegium Nordicum" einst den Jesuiten. Von dieser Zeit kündet heute noch das Wappen mit den nordischen „Hl. Drei Königen": Erich von Schweden, Knut von Dänemark und Olaf von Norwegen. Heute heißt das Gebäude in der Bethlehemstraße 7 schlicht *Nordico* und beherbergt das Linzer Stadtmuseum.

Brunnen im Ursulinenhof. – Fountain in the Ursulinenhof.

Der westliche Linzer Brückenkopf. – The west Linz Brückenkopf.

Das Landeskulturzentrum Ursulinenhof. – The Provincial Culture Centre in Ursulinenhof.

A Cultural Centre for Everyone

Since 1680 the Ursulines in Landstrasse have been involved in education. When the order itself moved out of the building in 1968, the rooms were converted to other educational purposes, although they are a far cry from traditional schooling. The magnificent baroque building, built by Georg and Franz Pruckmayr in the years 1692–1697, was completely renovated in the 70's and was turned over to the public by the provincial government of Upper Austria in the form of the Cultural Centre Ursulinenhof. There is room for every sort of creative activity here. There is plenty of space for the thriving art life of Upper Austria. And the "cellar theatre" is available for experimental productions by the Landestheater.

A Monastery School for Northern Pupils

This was the purpose of the former "Collegium Nordico" run by the Jesuits. This is evident today when we view the coat of arms with its northern "Holy Three Kings": Erich of Sweden, Knut of Denmark and Olaf of Norway. The building in Bethlehemstrasse 7 is just called Nordico today and is the site of the City Museum of Linz.

Ein „vaterländisches Museum ob der Enns"

Das schwebte Anton Ritter von Spaun vor, als er 1833 den „Verein des vaterländischen Museums für Österreich ob der Enns" gründete, aus dem sich das heutige *Oberösterreichische Landesmuseum* entwickelte. Das Gebäude zählt zu den bedeutendsten Schöpfungen des österreichischen Historismus. Seinen Namen *Francisco Carolinum* verdankt es dem Erzherzog Franz Karl. Heute beherbergt das Bauwerk vor allem naturkundliche Sammlungen und oberösterreichische Malerei des 19. und 20. Jahrhunderts.

Zwischen Gustav Klimt und Alfred Kubin

Wer vor dem Hochhaus mit dem Namen *Lentia 2000* in der Urfahrer Blütenstraße 15 steht, der wird zunächst nicht daran denken, daß dieses Gebäude eine der bedeutendsten Kunstsammlungen Österreichs beherbergen könnte. Als solche kann man die *Neue Galerie der Stadt Linz* jedoch durchaus bezeichnen, die auf der Basis der berühmten Gurlitt-Sammlung entstanden ist. Auf einer Ausstellungsfläche von 2.300 m² sind 600 Gemälde und Plastiken, 3.500 Zeichnungen, Aquarelle und Druckgraphiken sowie 2.000 Reproduktionen von Meistern zu sehen, die etwa ab der Mitte des vorigen Jahrhunderts gewirkt haben. Ein besonderes Gustostückerl der Galerie ist das Kubin-Kabinett mit rund 600 graphischen Blättern des eigenwilligen Künstlers aus Zwickledt.

A "Fatherland Museum for the Land above the Enns"

This was the idea of Anton Ritter von Spaun when he founded the "Society for a Fatherland Museum for the Land above the Enns" in 1833. Today it is simply called Oberösterreichisches Landesmuseum, the Upper Austrian Provincial Museum. The building ranks among the most significant examples of the style known as "historicism". Archduke Franz Karl is responsible for the name of the building, Francisco Carolinum. Today it houses administration offices as well as the natural history collections and Upper Austrian paintings of the 19th and 20th centuries.

From Gustav Klimt to Alfred Kubin

If you stand in front of the high rise with the name Lentia 2000 in Urfahrer Blütenstrasse 15, you will probably not imagine that it houses one of the most significant collections of art in Austria. This is, however, the apt description for the New Gallery of the City of Linz which has grown from the basis provided by the famous Gurlitt-Collection. Six hundred paintings and sculptures, 3,500 drawings, water colours and prints as well as 2,000 reproductions can be seen in its 2,300 m² area from masters who worked during the middle of the last century. A special attraction is the Kubin Cabinet which contains 600 graphic works by this headstrong artist from Zwickledt.

Gegenüberliegende Seite: Landesmuseum Francisco Carolinum.
Opposite page: Provincial museum Francisco Carolinum.

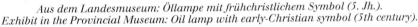

Aus dem Landesmuseum: Öllampe mit frühchristlichem Symbol (5. Jh.).
Exhibit in the Provincial Museum: Oil lamp with early-Christian symbol (5th century).

Ausstellungsräume im Oberösterreichischen Landesmuseum mit Exponaten von Oliver Dorfer und Ona B.
Exhibition rooms in the Upper Austrian Provincial Museum with objects by Oliver Dorfer and Ona B.

Links: Das „Adalbert Stifter Haus" an der Donaulände 6.
Left: The "Adalbert Stifter House" at Donaulände 6.
Rechts: Haus der „k.k. Privaten Ersten Eisenbahngesellschaft" (1832) in Urfahr.
Right: House of the "First Imperial and Royal Railway" (1832) in Urfahr.

Klinke an Adalbert Stifters Wohnhaus. – Brick on Adalbert Stifter's house.

Wo Stifter lebte

Wenn Anton Bruckner in Linz der musikalische Genius loci ist, so ist es Adalbert Stifter auf dem Gebiet der Literatur. Er hat sich übrigens nicht nur um die Literatur, sondern auch um viele Kunstschätze seiner Heimat, etwa den berühmten Kefermarkter Altar, verdient gemacht. Von 1846 bis zu seinem Tod im Jahre 1868 lebte Stifter in einem Biedermeierhaus an der Unteren Donaulände 6, wo heute nicht nur ein Gedenkraum, sondern auch das *Adalbert-Stifter-Institut* untergebracht ist.

Was aus den Klosterbibliotheken entstand

Die zahlreichen, zum großen Teil von Josef II. aufgehobenen Klöster verfügten allesamt über recht eindrucksvolle Bibliotheksbestände. Sie bilden die Grundlage der heutigen *Studienbibliothek* am Schillerplatz, die mittlerweile etwa 300.000 Bände umfaßt.

Where Stifter lived

If Anton Bruckner is the Genius loci in the field of music then Adalbert Stifter fills that role for literature. His own field of activity did not confine itself to literature, however, but included many of the arts of his homeland – in his concern for the famous Altar at Kefermarkt, for example. From 1846 until his death in the year 1868, Stifter lived in a Biedermeier house at Untere Donaulände 6. Today, his former residence houses not only a commemorative room, but also the Adalbert Stifter Institute.

The Wealth of the Convent Libraries

The many convents which were disolved by Emperor Josef II contained a vast wealth of books. They formed the basis for today's Studienbibliothek, *or scholar's library, on Schillerplatz which comprises around 300,000 volumes.*

Aus der Studienbibliothek: Weltdarstellung aus der Historia Scholastica (13. Jh.) aus dem Stift Baumgarten.
Scholar's library: Portrayal of the world from Historia Scholastica (13th century) in the Baumgarten Convent.

MODERNES LINZ
Modern Linz

Yachthafen und Ruderbecken. – Yacht harbour and rowing pool.

Durch den Rhein-Main-Donau-Kanal hat der Linzer Hafen noch an Bedeutung gewonnen.
The harbour of Linz became even more important with the completion of the Rhein-Main-Danube Canal.

Durch den Einsatz von Kraft-Wärme-Kopplung ist das ESG Fernheizkraftwerk Linz-Süd eines der umweltfreundlichsten in Europa.
Thanks to the use of deployed industrial heat, the ESG district heating system is one of the most environment-friendly in Europe.

Industriestadt Linz

Daß sich Linz von einer kleinen mittelalterlichen Stadt zu einer stetig aufstrebenden Metropole entwickelte, verdankt es vor allem dem Fleiß seiner Bevölkerung in Handel und Industrie. Die Wollzeugfabrik, die von Christian Sint 1672 als erste Textilfabrik Mitteleuropas erbaut wurde, ist nur einer der vielen Meilensteine, die zur heutigen Industriestadt Linz geführt haben. Vor allem denkt man bei diesem Schlagwort an zwei Betriebe: die *Austrian Industries AG* und die *OMV-Gruppe.* Letztere, aus den ehemaligen „Stickstoffwerken" hervorgegangen, ist das bedeutendste chemische Industrieunternehmen Österreichs. Die Produktpalette reicht heute von Kunststoffen über Düngemittel bis zu Pharmazeutika.

Im Zentrum der Linzer Industrie steht indessen der Konzern *Austrian Industries AG*, mit ca. 80.000 Mitarbeitern der größte Arbeitgeber Österreichs. Die eigentliche Aufbauphase begann nach dem Anschluß an das „1000jährige Reich". Die „Partnerschaft des Führers" und den schnellen Aufbau der damaligen „Hermann-Göring-Werke" mußten die Linzer allerdings mit dem Bombenhagel der letzten Kriegsjahre bitter bezahlen.

Industrial Linz

The fact that Linz has developed from a small medieval town into a constantly expanding metropolis is due above all to the industriousness of its population in the trade and industry sector. The wool factory which was founded by Christian Sint in 1672, as the first textile factory in central Europe, is only one of the milestones of Linz's way to becoming the industrial city it is today. Of course, upon hearing the word, one thinks primarily of the two business enterprises: Austrian Industries AG *and the OMV Group. The latter, which used to be a nitre works, is Austria's most important chemical manufacturer. Today, its range of products includes synthetic materials, fertilisers and pharmaceutical products.*

The company Austrian Industries AG *stands at the centre of industrial life in Linz; employing some 80,000 people, it is the largest employer in Austria. The actual building work did not get underway until after the "Anschluss" of Austria with the "1,000 Year Reich". "The partnership with the Führer" and the quick development of what was then the "Hermann Göring Works" was bitterly paid for the people of Linz in the form of the hail of bombs which rained down on them during the last years of the war.*

Oben: Anlage der OMV-Gruppe. – Above: Grounds of the OMV Group.
Links unten: Mechanische Bearbeitung in der VOEST-ALPINE M.C.E. – Below left: Mechanical work at VOEST-ALPINE M.C.E.
Rechts unten: Bandbeschichtungsanlage der VOEST-ALPINE Stahl. – Below right: Industrial tape preparation plant of the VOEST-ALPINE.

Links unten: Der Linzer Werkshafen als Umschlagplatz für Masse und Klasse, also für Rohstoffe und Endprodukte von höchster Qualität.
Below left: The Linz harbour as a venue for mass-produced and high-class products, raw products and finished goods.

Oben: Die Hochofensilhouette im Linzer Werk der VOEST-ALPINE spiegelt sich im werkseigenen Hafen. – Above: Silhouette of the Linz VOEST-ALPINE blast furnace reflected in its own harbour.

Rechts unten: Die VOEST-ALPINE Stahl erzeugt hochwertige Bleche; Schmelztauchveredelungsanlage 2. – Below right: VOEST-ALPINE manufactures high-quality metals; smelter refinery 2.

Erstes COREX-Stahlwerk der Welt, entwickelt und gebaut von der VOEST-ALPINE Industrieanlagenbau Ges.m.b.H.
für die Firma ISCOR Limited, Südafrika.
The first COREX steel works in the world, developed and built by VOEST-ALPINE Industrial Construction Ges.m.b.H.
for the ISCOR Company Ltd. in South Africa.

Nach dem Zusammenbruch begann auch für die Linzer Stahlindustrie eine neue Aufbauphase. Das Werk wurde am 1. Oktober 1945 in „Vereinigte Österreichische Eisen- und Stahlwerke" (VOEST) umbenannt. 1952 begann eine neue Epoche in der österreichischen Industriegeschichte: Das nach dem Krieg in Linz und Donawitz entwickelte, neuartige LD-Verfahren fand nicht nur weltweite Beachtung, sondern führte zur Eröffnung des ersten LD-Stahlwerkes der Welt. Die VOEST zählte mit der betriebsreifen Anwendung dieses revolutionierenden Stahlerzeugungsverfahrens zu den modernsten „Stahlkochern" Europas, ja der ganzen Welt.

Aus dem reinen Stahlwerk entwickelte sich ein vielseitiger Industriekonzern, dieser wurde im Jahre 1989 in die *Austrian Industries AG* eingebunden. Die heutigen Linzer Konzerngesellschaften wie z. B. VOEST-ALPINE *Stahl*, VOEST-ALPINE *Industrieanlagenbau* und VOEST-ALPINE M.C.E. tragen maßgeblich dazu bei, den Ruf, den die „alte" VOEST im internationalen Wirtschaftsleben hat, weiter zu verbessern.

After the debacle, a new period of development began for the steel industry of Linz. On October 1st 1945 the factory was renamed the "Vereinigte Österreichische Eisen- und Stahlwerke" (United Austrian Iron and Steel Works), abbreviated to VOEST. In 1952 a new period of Austrian industrial history began. The new forms of LD process developed in Linz and Donawitz after the war led to the received international acclaim but also led to the opening of the first top blowing steelworks in the world. In applying this revolutionary new steel manufacturing process, the VOEST became one of the most modern steelworks in Europe, even in the whole world.

Out of the steelworks developed a many-sided enterprise which in 1989 became part of the Austrian Industries AG. *The present-day companies based in Linz, e.g. VOEST-ALPINE Steel, VOEST-ALPINE Industrial Construction and VOEST-ALPINE M.C.E., continue this tradition and make an important contribution to improving the good reputation that the "old" VOEST enjoys in the international business world.*

Der Linzer Stadthafen. – The Linz Municipal Harbour.

Die Johannes-Kepler-Universität Linz. Bibliotheksgebäude. – The Johannes Kepler University Linz. Library.

Mehr als drei Jahrhunderte nach Kepler

Linz verfügte stets über eine große wissen-
schaftliche Tradition. Nicht nur das berühmte
Jesuitengymnasium, vor allem auch das Wirken
Johannes Keplers sind dafür Beweis genug.
Dennoch brauchte es nach Keplers Tod im Jahre
1630 noch insgesamt 336 Jahre, bis Linz im
Jahre 1966 erhielt, was es in vergleichbaren
Städten meist schon seit Jahrhunderten gab:
Eine *Universität*, die ihren Namen wohl nur nach
Johannes Kepler erhalten konnte. Der Campus
wurde am Grünrand von Linz beim alten *Schloß
Auhof* errichtet und seither wegen des großen
Zustroms mehrfach erweitert.

More than Three Hundred Years after Kepler

*Linz has always been known for its long history
of scientific development. Not only the famous
Jesuit Secondary School but also the work of
Johannes Kepler is proof enough. Nevertheless, it
took 336 years after the death of Kepler in 1630 for
Linz to finally get in 1966 what similar cities had
already had for centuries: its very own* University.
*It was obvious that it would be named for Kepler.
The campus was set up on the green belt of Linz
near the old* Auhof Castle. *The demand for study
places was so great that it was soon expanded.*

Modernster Komfort für die Patienten im neu errichteten AKH.
Patients enjoy the most modern comfort in the new general hospital.

Wohnhausanlage auf dem Ennsfeld. – Apartment houses in Ennsfeld.

Linz mit neuem Antlitz

Vom schmucken Barockstädtchen an der Donau bis zum Industriezentrum hat Linz zahllose Phasen durchlaufen, in denen es sein Gesicht immer wieder geändert hat. Auch das Linz der Gegenwart hat sich eine eigene, unverkennbare Physiognomie geschaffen. Das gilt keineswegs nur für die Industriezone um den *Linzer Hafen* mit jährlich 5,5 Millionen Tonnen Umschlag, sondern auch für das übrige Linz, für dessen fortschrittliche Gesinnung vor allem die zukunftsorientierte Architektur des *Neuen Rathauses* am linken Ufer repräsentativ ist. Hier haben mit Ausnahme des Bürgermeisters, des Magistratspräsidiums und des Präsidialamts sämtliche Ämter der Gemeinde Linz ihren Sitz. Mit dem Neuen Rathaus ist es auf überzeugende Weise gelungen, ein modernes Bauwerk harmonisch in das Urfahrer Altstadtensemble einzubetten.

Wohnanlagen, Sportstätten, Banken, Hotels und Skulpturen in moderner Stahl- und Glasarchitektur scheinen für das Linz der Gegenwart zu sein, was barocke Zwiebelturmhelme für die Vergangenheit waren.

Im neuen *Ars Electronica Center* am Urfahrer Brückenkopf kann man gar in eine dreidimensionale Computerwelt eintauchen und sich darin bewegen. Cybercity Linz, die digitale Stadt der Zukunft – Städteplanung auf dem Computer wird anhand eines aktuellen Linzer Großbauvorhabens, der „Solar City Pichling", demonstriert.

A New Face for Linz

From a jewel-like baroque city on the Danube to an industrial centre, Linz has gone through a great many phases in which her appearance has been constantly changing. Contemporary Linz has also taken on its very own, unmistakeable physiognomy. This is not only only true of the industrial zone around the Linz Harbour which has over 5.5 million tons turnover annually, but also for the rest of the town. A highly up-date feeling for the spirit of the times and for future-oriented architecture led to the construction of the Neue Rathaus – New City Hall – on the left bank of the river. Aside from the office of the mayor, the town council and a few other authorities, the entire administration has its seat here.

The New City Hall is a sterling example of contemporary architecture which blends harmoniously with the surrounding historical buildings. Apartment houses, sport fields, banks, hotels and sculptures in modern glass and steel construction represent present-day Linz, just as the baroque onion domes did in past times.

In the new Ars Electronica Center on Urfahrer Brückenkopf, one can even enter a three-dimensional computer world. Cybercity Linz, the digital city of the future, illustrates the practical application of city planning with computers, demonstrated by the current major building plans for "Solar City Pichling".

Gegenüberliegende Seite oben: Blick vom Linzer Schloß auf das Neue Rathaus in Urfahr.
Opposite page above: View of the Urfahr City Hall from the Castle of Linz.

Jubiläumsbrunnen. – Jubilee Fountain.

Seniorenheim in der Glimpfingerstraße. – Senior citizens' home in Glimpfingerstrasse.

Tabakfabrik, nach Entwurf von Peter Behrens und Alexander Popp 1929/35 erbaut. – Tobacco factory, built from a design by Peter Behrens and Alexander Popp 1929/35.

Oben: Dachterrasse des „Neuen Rathauses". – Above: Roof terrace of the "New City Hall".
Unten: City-Einkaufszentrum „Arkade". – Below: City-shopping centre "Arkade".

Blick vom Pöstlingberg auf Linz. – View of Linz from Pöstlingberg.

Oben: Seniorenheim Dauphinestraße. – Above: Senior citizens' home in Dauphinestrasse.
Unten: Menschenrechtsbrunnen in der Seilerstätte. – Below: Fountain of Human Rights in Seilerstätte.

Oben: Eingangsportal des Posthofs 2. – Above: Entrance portal of Posthof 2.
Unten: Maxx Hotel an der Donaulände. – Below: Maxx Hotel on the banks of the Danube.

Das Erlebnisbad Hummelhof. – Experience bath Hummelhof.
Gegenüberliegende Seite oben: Das Parkbad. Mitte: Ruderer in Aktion. Unten: Das Linzer Stadion auf der Gugl.
Opposite page above: The Park Baths. Middle: Rowers in action. Below: The stadium of Linz on the Gugl.

GRÜNES LINZ
Green Linz

Aphroditetempel auf dem Freinberg. – The Temple of Aphrodite on Freinberg.
Gegenüberliegende Seite: Promenadenweg auf dem Freinberg.
Opposite page: Promenade on Freinberg.

95

Oben und unten: Skulpturen der Linzer Kunsthochschule, des „Forum Metall", im Donaupark.
Above and below: Sculptures of the Linz College of Fine Arts, the "Forum Metall", in the Danube Park.

Luftkurort – bitte warten ...

Seit 1985 arbeitet die Stadt Linz in Zusammen-
arbeit mit der Industrie erfolgreich an einem
Luftkonzept. Der Schadstoffausstoß konnte
seither immerhin um fast 75% reduziert werden.
Linz ist zwar noch kein Luftkurort, aber es wird
weiter daran gearbeitet!

A Fresh Air Zone – Please Wait a Little ...

*The City of Linz has been working together with
its industries since 1985 on a new fresh air programme. Pollution has already been reduced by
75%. While Linz may still not be a "fresh air
zone", the town and its inhabitants are hard at
work to make it one.*

Grüne Lungen in der Stadt

Zu den schönsten dieser „grünen Lungen" zählt der *Volksgarten* an der Landstraße, zwischen Blumau und Goethestraße. Er wurde bereits zu Beginn des 19. Jahrhunderts vom Kaffeehausbesitzer Bartholomäus Festorazzi angelegt. 1857 kaufte die Stadtgemeinde den Park, um ihn vor der drohenden Verbauung zu schützen. Um die Jahrhundertwende war der Volksgarten ein beliebtes Vergnügungszentrum mit einem großen Saal, der allerdings durch einen Bombentreffer im Zweiten Weltkrieg zerstört wurde. Ein Denkmal im Volksgarten erinnert an den Dichter der oberösterreichischen Nationalhymne „Hoamatland", Franz Stelzhamer.
Auch der *Promenadenpark* birgt das Denkmal eines oberösterreichischen Dichters. In der Grünanlage, die an der Stelle der 1800 abgetragenen Stadtmauer entstand, schuf der Wiener

Green Lungs in the City

One of the most beautiful of these so-called "green lungs" is the Volksgarten – *literally, People's Garden – on Landstrasse, between Blumau and Goethestrasse. It was laid out at the beginning of the 19th century by the coffee house owner Bartholomäus Festorazzi. In 1857, the city of Linz bought the park in order to protect it from impending development. At the turn of the century it provided a number of attractions including a multi-purpose hall which was unfortunately destroyed during the Second World War. A commemorative plaque in the Volksgarten is dedicated to the author of the Upper Austrian anthem "Hoamatland", Franz Stelzhamer.*
Promenadenpark *also contains a memorial to a local poet. This park grew on the site of the city walls which were torn down in 1800 and here the*

Blick auf die Altstadt vom Bauernberg. – View of the Old Town from Bauernberg.

Das Jesuitenkolleg auf dem Freinberg. – The Jesuit College on Freinberg.
Gegenüberliegende Seite: Adalbert-Stifter-Denkmal auf der Promenade.
Opposite page: Adalbert Stifter Monument on the Promenade.

Bildhauer Hans Rathausky ein Denkmal Adalbert Stifters.

Besonders gut ist in Linz in den letzten Jahrzehnten die Einbettung des Donaustroms in das Stadtbild gelungen. Dazu tragen nicht nur Brucknerhaus und Rathaus bei, sondern auch der große *Donaupark*, zwischen dessen schönen Blumenrabatten und großen Rasenflächen moderne Plastiken der Dauerausstellung „Forum Metall" für einen avantgardistischen Blickfang sorgen.

Zu den kleineren Innenstadt-Parks, in denen man auf einer Parkbank für eine Weile der Großstadt-Hektik entfliehen kann, zählen auch der *Hessenplatz* mit dem schönen Neptunbrunnen, der früher am Hauptplatz zu Hause war, sowie der *Schillerpark*, den seit ein paar Jahren eine moderne Springbrunnenanlage ziert, die an heißen Tagen für etwas Abkühlung sorgt. Natürlich laden auch die ausgedehnten Parkanlagen am *Schloßberg* mit ihrem schönen Ausblick über die Dächer von Linz zum Verweilen ein.

Viennese sculptor Hans Rathausky carved a monument to Adalbert Stifter.

Within recent years, the Danube itself has been actively incorporated into the cityscape of Linz. This is thanks not only to the Bruckner House and the New City Hall, but also to the large Danube Park, *which offers not only beautiful flower beds and vast lawns, but also modern sculptures and a permanent exhibition called "Forum Metall" which provides an eyecatching avant-garde note.*

Then there are the small parks in the city centre where a few moments of peace and quiet can be snatched in the midst of hectic city life. There is Hessenplatz (Hessen Square) with its beautiful Neptune Fountain, which was moved here from the Main Square, or Schillerpark with its modern fountain whose soaring waters offer a bit of refreshment on sultry days. Finally, there are the spacious gardens of Schlossberg, Castle Hill, *with their splendid view over the roofs of Linz which lure one to enjoy a few peaceful moments of relaxation.*

Franz-Josephs-Warte auf dem Freinberg. – Franz-Josephs-Warte on Freinberg.

Denkmal der Pferdeeisenbahn Linz – Budweis. – The Linz – Budweis Horse-drawn Train Monument.

Pferdeeisenbahnpromenade. – Horse-drawn Train Promenade.

Bergschlößlpark. – Bergschlösslpark.

Gute Luft an der Peripherie

Wenn man vom Hessenplatz mit dem Obus
Richtung Bindermichlkirche fährt, so findet man
zwischen Vorstadthäusern und Stadtumfahrun-
gen unversehens ein kleines Wäldchen, welches
das Stadtbild freundlich auflockert. Der *Hummelhofwald* ist seit jeher für die Linzer Bevölkerung
eine Art Freizeitparadies. Hier läßt sich's im
Sommer im Freibad planschen. Wer Zeit hat,
kann auch an einem der beiden Freiluftschach-
bretter den feindlichen König matt setzten.
Erst in jüngster Zeit wurde auch das riesige
Areal des *Wasserwaldes* bei Kleinmünchen für die
Bevölkerung weitgehend freigegeben. Die weit-
läufige Anlage erinnert mit ihren großen Rasenflächen ein wenig an den Londoner Hyde Park.
Hier ist ein Zentrum für sonntägliche Familien-
Picknicks, Jogging-Fans, Radfahrer, winterliche
Langläufer und Rodelfahrer geschaffen worden.

Fresh Air on the Periphery

*If you take the O-bus from Hessen Square in the
direction marked Bindermichlkirche, you will find
a little woods nestled between the suburban houses
and the access roads which contributes its part in
making the surroundings attractive. It is called
Hummelhofwald and it has always been a sort of
leisure time paradise for the people of Linz. In
summer there is an open-air bathing area here
and whoever has the time can try to manœuvre
the enemy king into checkmate on one of the over-
sized chess boards.*
*Recently, another small forest has been opened to
the public – the Wasserwald near Kleinmünchen.
This spacious area with its vast lawns reminds
one a bit of Hyde Park in London. It is the destination of families with picnics, joggers and cross
country skiers and sledders in winter.*
The industrialist Ludwig Hatschek is to thank for

101

Impressionen aus dem Botanischen Garten. – Impressions from the Botanical Gardens.

Erholungslandschaft Wasserwald-Park. – Recreation Centre Wasserwald Park.

Eine etwas hügeligere Freizeitoase bieten die auf Initiative des Großindustriellen Ludwig Hatschek geschaffenen Parkanlagen am *Bauernberg* und *Auf der Gugl* den Linzern an. Sie wurden schon 1885 angelegt. Und die Parkgestaltung vermag diverse klassizistische Züge auch nicht zu verleugnen. So findet man hier etwa einen ionischen Aphroditetempel, der aus dem 19. Jahrhundert stammt. Die Terrasse auf dem abschließenden Plateau ist ein beliebter Aussichtstreff der Linzer. Auf dem Bauernberg befindet sich auch das Linzer Stadion, eines der modernsten Kleinstadien Europas. Nicht nur der Fußball regiert hier – das jährliche „Gugl-Meeting" ist zu einem fixen Termin im internationalen Leichtathletikkalender geworden.

Man kann ein Kapitel über „das grüne Linz" indessen nicht beenden, ohne den berühmten *Botanischen Garten* zu erwähnen. Ein Vorläufer entstand schon um 1750 beim Bergschlößl, aber erst 1950 erhielt dieses naturhistorische Linzer Juwel eine entsprechend große Fläche von 4,2 ha, auf der all die vielen heimischen und exotischen Gewächse zwischen Seerosenteichen, Sonnenterrassen und Rosarien erst so richtig zur Wirkung gelangen können.

Die Heilhamer Au. – Heilhamer Marsh.

a hilly recreation area where you will find the parks Bauernberg *and* Auf der Gugl. *They were laid out in 1885, and their planning betrays certain neo-classic elements. There is an ionic temple to Aphrodite, for example. The terrace on the plateau above is a favourite meeting point of day trippers. On Bauernberg is the Stadium of Linz, one of the most modern small stadiums of Europe. But it is a venue not only for football: it is the site of the annual "Gugl Meeting" which is a popular meeting point for fans of light-athletics from all over the world.*

It would not be possible to end a chapter on "the green Linz" without mentioning the famous Botanical Garden. *In its first form, it was laid out in 1750 near the Bergschlössl, but it was not until 1950 that this superb garden expanded to its full size of 4.2 hectares in which many indigenous and exotic varieties of plant life luxuriate. The lily ponds, sun terraces and rose gardens can now be enjoyed to the full.*

Rechts: Parkanlage auf dem Bauernberg.
Right: Park landscape on Bauernberg.

LINZ UND DIE LINZER
Linz and her people

Die berühmte Linzer Torte. – The famous Linz Torte.
Gegenüberliegende Seite: Der Hauptplatz mit der Dreifaltigkeitssäule.
Opposite page: The Main Square with its Holy Trinity Column.

Die schöne Linzerin

„Dir mit Wohlgeruch zu kosen,
Deine Freuden zu erhöhen,
Knospend müssen tausend Rosen
Erst in Gluten untergehn."

Diese schönen Verse sind für eine „schöne Linzerin" geschrieben worden. Der Dichter ist kein Geringerer als der alte Geheimrat Goethe. Und an die so bilderreich Angebetete erinnert heute noch ein Steinporträt am Linzer Pfarrplatz im Haus Nr. 4. Lange Zeit nahm man an, daß dort jene Marianne von Willemer zur Welt gekommen ist, die Goethe als Suleika in seinem „West-

The Lovely Girl from Linz

*"To even approach your fragrance
Or to touch your special charms
The buds of a thousand roses
Must be committed to the flames."*

These romantic verses were written for a "beautiful maiden of Linz". The poet was none other than Johann Wolfgang von Goethe. And just such a beauty can be seen in stone relief on the house at Linzer Pfarrplatz Nr. 4. For many years one assumed that this was the birthplace of Marianne von Willemer, immortalized by Goethe as Suleika in his "West-östlichen Divan". Is it a mere coincidence

Shopping im City-Einkaufszentrum „Arkade" am Taubenmarkt.
Shopping in the City-shopping centre "Arkade" on Taubenmarkt.

Buntes Angebot auf dem Südbahnhofmarkt. – Colourful offers at the Südbahn Market.

östlichen Divan" verewigt hat. Ist es ein Zufall, daß gerade dieser Inbegriff weiblicher Anmut und Schönheit eine Linzerin war? – Offenbar nicht. Denn die Erfahrungen Goethes haben noch zahlreiche andere Poeten und Dichter gemacht, die „die schöne Linzerin" immer wieder hymnisch gepriesen haben. Benedikt Pillwein hielt es sogar für nötig, seiner „Geschichte der Stadt Linz" ein Kapitel einzuverleiben, in dem „die Frauenzimmer in Linz" einer genaueren Erläuterung unterzogen werden. „Geschaffen, das menschliche Daseyn zu verschönern und mitzugenießen, finden sich die hiesigen Frauenzimmer im Theater, in Konzerten, beim Spiele und bei anderen fröhlichen Zusammenkünften der Männer ein, wodurch der gesellschaftliche Umgang in Linz sehr gewinnt." Und weiter meint der Stadthistorikus: „Die schönen Linzerinnen; so wollte und will man dadurch nicht bloß die Eingeborenen bezeichnen, sondern auch aussprechen, daß hier der größte Zusammenfluß vom schönen Geschlechte aus Oberösterreich zu treffen sey."

that this apothesis of feminine beauty and charm was a resident of Linz? – Probably not. For what Goethe experienced has also been noted by countless poets and writers who have sung the praises of the women of the town. Benedikt Pillwein found it necessary to add a special chapter to his "History of the City of Linz" in which the "womenvolk of Linz" are described in some detail. "They were created to make our lot in life a bit more beautiful and such womenfolk may be found in the theatre, at concerts and at various pastimes and other pleasant pursuits which means a fine advantage for social life in Linz." The scribe continues: "The beauties of Linz – by which I do not mean only those who are native to this fair city, but all those ladies who have gravitated naturally to the capital from all parts of Upper Austria."

Der traditionsreiche Südbahnhofmarkt. – The traditional Südbahn Market.

Seit 1817 findet jährlich im Frühjahr und Herbst der vielbesuchte Urfahrer Jahrmarkt statt.
The popular Urfahr County Fair has been held in spring and autumn since 1817.

Flohmarkt am Hauptplatz.
Fleamarket on the Main Square.

Ganz in Gold ...

Es gibt kaum eine größere Festivität in Linz und Umgebung, wo sie nicht blitzen würden: die kunstvollen *Linzer Goldhauben,* die im Lauf der letzten drei Jahrhunderte sicherlich zum anerkannten Ruf der „schönen Linzerin" beigetragen haben. Die Goldhaube ist vielen Linzerinnen äußeres Zeichen einer tiefen Verbundenheit zu Tradition und Brauchtum ihrer Heimat: Dazu trägt man Dirndlkleider, die mehr oder weniger der klassischen oberösterreichischen Nationaltracht mit der eng taillierten schwarzen Samtjacke und der ebenfalls schwarzen Seidenschürze über einem bauschigen Rock entsprechen.

Linzer Symphonie aus Mürbteig

An den angeblichen Erfinder der Linzer Torte erinnert heute noch die *Johann-Konrad-Vogel-Straße.* Die wenigsten Linzer wissen sie heute noch mit dem Namen jenes berühmten Zuckerbäckers zu verbinden, der im Jahre 1822 aus Weihenzell nach Linz zog und von dort ein „Geheimrezept" mitbrachte, das sich in Linz schlagartig zum absoluten Mehlspeis-Hit entwickelte und es bis heute geblieben ist.

Beliebt sind Speis und Trank in den Gastgärten der Linzer Mostbauern.
The Linz cider makers are known for their food and drink.

All in Gold ...

*No greater festivity in Linz or its surroundings
would be complete without them, the intricate,
elaborate gold bonnets of Linz which have cer-
tainly done their part over the last three centuries
to enhance the reputation of the beauties of Linz.
For many women of Linz, the gold bonnet is a
symbol of their deep relationship with the tradition and customs of their homeland. The suitable
dress to go with them is the Austrian "Dirndl"
which is the more or less classic Upper Austrian
folk costume consisting of a tailored black velvet
jacket and a black silk apron over a wide cut
skirt.*

A Symphony in Pastry

*The alleged inventor of the speciality is com-
memorated by a street name:* Johann-Konrad-
Vogel-Strasse. *Very few residents realize that it
refers to the famous confectioner who moved to
Linz in 1822 from Weihenzell and brought a
"secret recipe" with him which immediately
became the "dessert-hit" it has remained to this
day.*

Linzer Goldhaube aus der Biedermeierzeit. – This golden bonnet is from the Biedermeier period.

Aper is'!

Das *Aperschnalzen* findet, untermalt von den Klängen der Turmbläser des Landhauses, alle Jahre wieder am Neujahrstag um elf Uhr vormittags auf der Linzer Promenade statt. Dieser typische Linzer Brauch geht schon auf heidnische Vorzeit zurück. „Aper" heißt im oberösterreichischen Dialekt soviel wie „leer, unbedeckt". Der Schnee, so will man mit diesem Brauch ausdrücken, soll nun die Erde wieder freigeben. Das neue Erntejahr kann beginnen.

Böllerschießen während des Aperschnalzens. – Fire crackers during the Aperschnalzen.

112

Landschaft im Kürnberger Wald. – Landscape in Kürnberger Woods.

"Aper is'!"

The Aperschnalzen *takes place every year on New Year's Day at 11 o'clock on the Promenade, accompanied by festive horn blowing from the towers of the Assembly House. It is a typical pagan custom which has survived until today.*
The word itself is an untranslatable dialect word meaning roughly "to whip away" or "whip clear" referring to a pagan custom of clearing away the snow so that the earth will be ready for spring. The new harvest year can begin.

Aperschnalzen – Tradition am Neujahrstag. – Aperschnalzen – tradition on New Year's Day.

LAND UM LINZ
The surroundings of Linz

Eingangsportal des Stiftes St. Florian.
Entrance portal of St. Florian's Monastery.
Gegenüberliegende Seite: Detail im Stiftshof St. Florian.
Opposite page: Detail from the courtyard of St. Florian's.

Blick vom Freinberg. – View from Freinberg.

Der Hausberg der Linzer

Es ist noch gar nicht so lange her, da war der Linzer *Pöstlingberg* für die Linzer ein von dichtem „Urwald" bestandener Bergrücken. Erst im 18. Jahrhundert sorgte ein Gnadenbild der Muttergottes, das an einem Baum befestigt war, für Legendenbildungen und Wunderheilungen. Die Errichtung großer Wallfahrtskirchen entsprach damals dem Zeitgeist. Und so wurde in den Jahren 1738 bis 1748 im Auftrag der Starhemberger von den Baumeistern Johann Haslinger und Johann Matthias Krinner die vielleicht schönste barocke Wallfahrtskirche Oberösterreichs errichtet.

Man erreichte sie über einen heute noch begehbaren, steilen Kreuzweg. Bald waren es jedoch nicht nur fromme Pilger, sondern auch die ersten Touristen eines neuen Zeitalters, die den Pöstlingberg als Reiseziel mit wunderschöner Aussicht entdeckten. Berghotels und Gasthöfe entstanden. Und am 29. Mai 1898 wurde ein eisenbahntechnisches Unikum eröffnet, das bis heute in Betrieb ist: Die steilste Adhäsionsbahn Europas, die trotz Steigungen von 10,5 Prozent ohne Zahnräder auskommt. Der Bergbahnhof ist in einen der vielen Festungstürme am Pöstlingberg

The Local Mountain

Not so long ago, the little mountain called Pöstlingberg seemed to the people of Linz to be a thick "jungle" of dense foliage. In the 18th century, a votive picture of the virgin Mary, attached to a tree, gave rise to legends of miracles and wonderous cures. In those days, pilgrimage churches were usually built on such sites and between 1738 and 1748, the master builders Johann Haslinger and Johann Matthias Krinner built what may well be the most beautiful pilgrimage church in Upper Austria, working under contract from the Starhemberg family.

It was reached by a steep path marked by the stations of the cross which is still intact. But soon not only the devout made their way to the beautiful church but also the first tourists of the new age of travel and leisure who made the Pöstlingberg their destination in order to enjoy its superb views. Mountain hotels and inns soon sprang up. And on the 29th of May, 1898, a unique sort of railway was opened which has remained in service to this day: the steepest adhesion railway in Europe, which despite an incline of 10.5 percent can make the trip up the mountain without cogs. The little station is housed in one of the many

Die Pöstlingbergbahn – steilste Adhäsionbahn Europas. – The Pöstlingberg Railway – the oldest adhesion railway of Europe.

integriert, die in der nachnapoleonischen Zeit als letztes Bollwerk vor Wien angelegt worden waren. Die Befestigungstürme, den Linzern als „Pulvertürme" vertraut, haben heute die verschiedensten Funktionen. Sie dienen als Aussichtswarten oder wurden in Villen und Ateliers umgebaut. Und in einem davon ist eine Hauptattraktion für Kinder untergebracht: die *Märchengrottenbahn*. Beliebt ist der Pöstlingberg auch für kleine Wanderungen, die man von Urfahr aus zurücklegen kann. Sie führen meist bei den *Urfahrwänd* vorbei, wo es einen Lehrtiergarten und Streichelzoo für Kinder gibt.

defensive towers which were built on the Pöstlingberg in the post-napoleonic era as the last bulwark before Vienna. The towers, called "powder towers" by the locals, have a number of different functions nowadays. Some simply boast splendid look-out points, others have been turned into villas or studios. And one is a main attraction for children: the Märchengrottenbahn.
*The mountain is also a popular goal for short hikes which can begin in the suburb "Urfahr".
At Urfahrwänd, there is an educational zoo and one where children can pet the animals themselves.*

Der Stiftshof in Wilhering. – The monestary courtyard in Wilhering.

Ein Prälatengarten aus dem Biedermeier
Im Zisterzienserstift *Wilhering*, 9 km westlich
von Linz, kommen sowohl Kunst- als auch Natur-
freunde auf ihre Rechnung. Die Kunstfreunde
werden eine der schönsten Stiftskirchen des
Rokoko bewundern, die in den Jahren 1734 bis
1750 von Johann Haslinger und Andreas Altomonte gebaut wurde, der gemeinsam mit Bartolomeo Altomonte auch für die malerische Aus-
gestaltung des Gotteshauses sorgte. Die Stiftskirche – heute ebenso wie die Wallfahrtskirche
am Pöstlingberg eine beliebte „Hochzeitskirche"
der Linzer – ist Maria Himmelfahrt geweiht und

A Prelate's Biedermeier Garden
The Cistercian convent Wilhering, *9 kilometres*
west of Linz, is a magnet for art lovers and
nature lovers alike. To begin with, it boasts one
of the most beautiful churches of the rococo which
was built between 1734 and 1750 by Johann
Haslinger and Andreas Altomonte, with paintings
by Bartolomeo Altomonte. This church, together
with the pilgrimage church of Pöstlingberg, is
very popular for local weddings. It is consecrated
to the Ascension and its foundations can be traced
back to 1146. The Cistercians were also especially
active in the field of education and Wilhering

Stift Wilhering. Hochaltar nach Entwurf von Andreas Altomonte. – Wilhering Monastery. High altar designed by Andreas Altomonte.

Blick auf die große Orgel in der Stiftskirche. – View of the great organ in the Stiftskirche.

geht auf eine Klostergründung aus dem Jahre 1146 zurück. Besondere Verdienste haben sich die Zisterzienser auch auf dem Gebiet der Erziehung erworben: Wilhering verfügt über ein eigenes Stiftsgymnasium.

Der Naturfreund wird sich indessen an dem im Biedermeier angelegten *Prälatengarten* gar nicht satt sehen können. Er gilt als schönster Stiftsgarten Österreichs und vereinigt Elemente französischer Barockgärten mit solchen des natürlich wuchernden „englischen Gartens" der Romantik. Ob Seerosenteich oder tausendjährige Eibe, Zwergpalme oder Tulpenbaum – hier macht die Natur tatsächlich aufsehenerregende Sprünge.

boasts its own secondary school.
Those with a taste for garden architecture will be fascinated by the so-called Prelate's Garden *which was laid out in the Biedermeier era. It has been called the most beautiful convent garden in Austria and combines elements of the French baroque with the romantic, "untamed gardens" of the English. Here, nature seems at its most capricious as you wander past the lily pond, the thousand year old yew tree, the miniature palms and the tulip tree.*

St. Florian. Großer Stiftshof mit dem Adlerbrunnen. – St. Florian's. The courtyard and Eagle Fountain.

St. Florian: Von Prandtauer bis Bruckner

Nur etwa 15 km südöstlich von Linz liegt eines der schönsten Barockstifte Österreichs. Seit 1071 sind in *St. Florian* die Augustinerchorherren ansässig. Der Grundstein zur monumentalen barocken Stiftsanlage wurde 1686 gelegt. Mit dem Bau beauftragte man zunächst den Italiener Carlo Carlone, der den Grundriß des berühmten Westtraktes schuf. Ihm folgte der Melker Stiftsbaumeister Jakob Prandtauer, zu dessen Meisterwerken vor allem die Vollendung des arkadengeschmückten *Stiegenhauses*, der prunkvolle, im Angedenken an den Sieg über die Türken errichtete *Marmorsaal* sowie das unweit von St. Florian gelegene Lustschloß barocker Kirchenfürsten, *Hohenbrunn* (heute ein Jagdmuseum), zählen.

Mit der „Karriere" des hl. Florian als Schutzpatron gegen die Feuersgefahr wurde das Stift bald zum beliebten Wallfahrtsort. Auch heute zieht es dank seiner großartigen Kunstschätze

St. Florian: From Prandtauer to Bruckner

Fifteen kilometres south-east of Linz is one of the most beautiful baroque monasteries of Austria. The Augustines have been home in St. Florian *since 1071. The cornerstone for this monumental baroque building was laid in 1686. First, the Italian Carlo Carlone was given the contract and he designed the floor plan for the famous west wing. He was succeeded by the master builder of the Monastery at Melk, Jakob Prandtauer. He was responsible for the arcaded staircase, the magnificent* Marble Hall *which commemorates the victory over the Turks as well as the pleasure palace of the clergy of the times,* Hohenbrunn, *which today houses a hunting museum.*

St. Florian is the patron saint of fire fighters and the monastery soon became a favourite place of pilgrimage. Today, the Imperial Apartments *attract thousands of visitors as does the famous* Altdorf Altar *which can be seen in the art collection. Finally, St. Florian is famous for its* Bruckner

Stift St. Florian – St. Florian's.

Stiftshof, im Hintergrund der Marmorsaal. – Monastery court-yard, in the background, the Marble Hall.

Abschlußgitter in der Stiftskirche. – Grating in the Stiftskirche.

in den *Kaiserzimmern* und wegen des berühmten *Altdorfer-Altars*, der in der Kunstsammlung zu sehen ist, jährlich unzählige Menschen an. Nicht zuletzt kommen sie auch, um die *Bruckner-Orgel* zu bewundern, die Wirkungsstätte des großen Symphonikers, der hier in der Gruft unter der Orgel begraben liegt.

Organ *which is named after the composer Anton Bruckner whose last resting place is located, appropiately, under this very organ.*

Darstellung des hl. Augustinus in einer Handschrift der Florianer Schreibschule aus der Stiftsbibliothek St. Florian.
Picture of St. Augustine in a manuscript in the monastery library of St. Florian's.

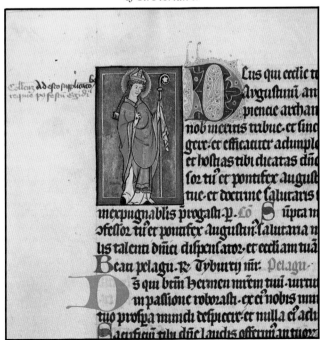

Die Ernte wird eingebracht. – Bringing in the harvest.

Balkonblumenschmuck in St. Florian. – Flowers on the balcony at St. Florian's.

Der Balkon von Linz

Wenn die Linzer an die frische Luft wollen, haben sie es nicht weit: In den beiden Orten *Hellmonsödt* und *Kirchschlag* können sie hoch oben auf den Mühlviertler Bergen ordentlich Luft tanken. Im Winter liegt hier zumeist viel Schnee, was die beiden Orte auch für Wintersportler attraktiv macht. In Hellmonsödt trifft der Kulturwanderer auf das volkskundlich besonders interessante *Freilichtmuseum Pelmberg*. Und in Kirchschlag kann er auf den Spuren Adalbert Stifters wandeln, an dessen ausgedehnte Aufenthalte unter der „Stifter-Linde" noch heute eine Gedenktafel an der Pfarrkirche erinnert.

Badespaß ist Trumpf

Ideal für heiße Tage sind Bäder wie etwa die *Erlebnisbäder Hummelhof* und *Schörgenhub*, das *Parkbad* an der Donau und eine ganze Palette von Badeseen rund um Linz. An schönen Sommertagen stürmt ganz Linz vor allem den *Pleschinger* und *Pichlinger See* sowie die *Feldkirchner Seen*, wo man in relativ warmem Wasser baden und sich in gepflegten Parkanlagen sonnen kann. Und im Winter geht's hinaus zum Eislaufen. Wie hat es doch Fritz von Herzmanovsky-Orlando so schön formuliert? – „Voll Kurzweil ist das Linzer Treiben – Drum auf nach Linz, und laßt uns dorten bleiben."

The Balcony of Linz

When the people of Linz want to get a bit of fresh air they do not have to go far: in the two villages of Hellmonsödt *and* Kirchschlag *they can refuel with oxygen high up in the mountains of the Mühlviertel range. There is usually a lot of snow here in winter, which makes both of these places popular for winter sports. In Hellmonsödt, travellers interested in cultural history will find the* open-air museum of Pelmberg *particularly interesting for its exhibition of folklore. And in Kirchschlag they can follow the tracks of the writer Adalbert Stifter, who often used to stay there.*

Bathing is Best

Ideal for hot days are the bathing spots around Linz, such as the Experience baths of Hummelhof *and* Schörgenhub, *the* Parkbad *on the Danube and a whole range of lakes. On fine summer days the people of Linz pour down to the* Pleschinger Lake, Pichlinger Lake *or* Feldkirchner Lakes, *where one can swim in the relatively warm water and sunbathe on beautiful laid-out grass areas.*
And in winter everybody goes out ice-skating. As Fritz von Herzmanovsky-Orlando so aptly put it: "Life in Linz is never, never dull – Let's off to Linz … and let's stay here!"

Gegenüberliegende Seite: Der Pleschinger See in Urfahr.
Opposite page: Pleschinger Lake in Urfahr.

LINZ AUF EINEN BLICK

Sehenswerte Sakralbauten

Martinskirche, Alter Dom, Maria-Empfängnis-Dom, Kapuzinerkirche, Ursulinenkirche, Karmeliterkirche, Seminarkirche, Elisabethinenkirche, Martin-Luther-Kirche, Kirche der Barmherzigen Brüder, Stadtpfarrkirche, Minoritenkirche, St. Michael (Bindermichl), St. Konrad (Froschberg), St. Theresia (Keferfeld)

Sehenswerte Profanbauten

Linzer Schloß, Landhaus, Bischofshof, Altes Rathaus, Hauptpostamt (ehemaliges Jesuitenkollegium, Domgasse 1), Palais Weissenwolf (Landstraße 12), Stiftshaus St. Florian (Landstraße 22), Klosterhof (Landstraße 30), Landeskulturzentrum Ursulinenhof (Landstraße 31), Starhembergisches Freihaus (Altstadt 17), Städtisches Waaghaus (Altstadt 12), Stiftshaus Kremsmünster (Altstadt 10), Freihaus Losenstein (Altstadt 2), Schloß Ebelsberg, Kaufmännisches Vereinshaus, Johannes-Kepler-Universität, Brucknerhaus, Stadion auf der Gugl, Design Center, Ars Electronica Center

Sehenswerte Straßen und Plätze

Hauptplatz, Tummelplatz, Alter Markt, Pfarrplatz, Landstraße, Taubenmarkt, Promenade, Herrenstraße, Altstadt, Klosterstraße, Domgasse, Hofberg

Museen

Schloßmuseum (Tummelplatz 10), Francisco Carolinum (Museumstraße 14), Stadtmuseum Nordico (Bethlehemstraße 7), Neue Galerie (Blütenstraße 15), Adalbert-Stifter-Gedenkraum (Untere Donaulände 6), Bischöfliches Diözesanmuseum (Kapuzinerstraße 84), Forum Metall

Parks und Gärten

Schloßpark, Volksgarten, Donaupark, Promenadenpark, Hessenplatzpark, Schillerpark, Park beim Neuen Dom, Andreas-Hofer-Park, Hummelhofpark, Bahnhofspark, Bauernberg, Auf der Gugl, Botanischer Garten, Wasserwald (Kleinmünchen)

Veranstaltungen

Internationales Brucknerfest, Linzer Klangwolke (September), Ars Electronica, Sommertheater im Schloßhof, Arkadenkonzerte im Linzer Landhaus (Sommersaison), Urfahrer Jahrmarkt, Linz-Fest, Pflasterspektakel

Theater

Linzer Landestheater (Großes Haus und Kammerspiele), Theaterkeller im Kulturzentrum Ursulinenhof, Linzer Kellertheater (Hauptplatz 33), Kinderkulturzentrum Kuddelmuddel (ehemaliges Kolpingkino, Langgasse 13), Posthof – Zeitkultur am Hafen, Theater Phönix, Offenes Kulturhaus

Bäder und Badeseen

Erlebnisbäder Hummelhof und Schörgenhub, Parkbad, Pichlinger See, Pleschinger See (teilweise FKK), Feldkirchner Seen, Weiklersee (FKK)

Flughafen

Linz Hörsching

Ausflugsziele rund um Linz

Pöstlingberg (Wallfahrtsbasilika und Märchengrottenbahn), Stift Wilhering, Kürnberger Wald, Stift St. Florian, Schloß Hohenbrunn, Tillysburg, Lichtenberg, Pesenbachtal, Hellmonsödt, Kirchschlag, Pferdeeisenbahnpromenade, Ansfelden (Bruckner-Geburtshaus), Lauriacum (Lorch), Kefermarkt (Altar, Schloß Weinberg), Donautal und Donauradweg

LINZ AT A GLANCE

Significant Sacral Buildings
Martinskirche, Alter Dom, Maria-Empfängnis-Dom, Kapuzinerkirche, Ursulinenkirche, Karmeliterkirche, Seminarkirche, Elisabethinenkirche, Martin-Luther-Kirche, Kirche der Barmherzigen Brüder, Stadtpfarrkirche, Minoritenkirche, St. Michael (Bindermichl), St. Konrad (Froschberg), St. Theresia (Keferfeld)

Significant Temporal Buildings
Linzer Schloss, Landhaus, Bischofshof, Altes Rathaus, Hauptpostamt (former Jesuitenkollegium, Domgasse 1), Palais Weissenwolf (Landstrasse 12), Stiftshaus St. Florian (Landstrasse 22), Klosterhof (Landstrasse 30), Landeskulturzentrum Ursulinenhof (Landstrasse 31), Starhembergisches Freihaus (Altstadt 17), Städtisches Waaghaus (Altstadt 12), Stiftshaus Kremsmünster (Altstadt 10), Freihaus Losenstein (Altstadt 2), Schloss Ebelsberg, Kaufmännisches Vereinshaus, Johannes-Kepler-Universität, Brucknerhaus, Stadion auf der Gugl, Design Center, Ars Electronica Center

Significant Sreets and Squares
Hauptplatz, Tummelplatz, Alter Markt, Pfarrplatz, Landstrasse, Taubenmarkt, Promenade, Herrenstrasse, Altstadt, Klosterstrasse, Domgasse, Hofberg

Museums
Schlossmuseum (Tummelplatz 10), Francisco Carolinum (Museumstrasse 4), Stadtmuseum Nordico (Bethlehemstrasse 7), Neue Galerie (Blütenstrasse 15), Adalbert-Stifter-Gedenkraum (Untere Donaulände 6), Bischöfliches Diözesanmuseum (Kapuzinerstrasse 84), Forum Metall

Parks and Gardens
Schlosspark, Volksgarten, Donaupark, Promenadenpark, Hessenplatzpark, Schillerpark, Park beim Neuen Dom, Andreas-Hofer-Park, Hummelhofpark, Bahnhofspark, Bauernberg, Auf der Gugl, Botanischer Garten, Wasserwald (Kleinmünchen)

Events
Internationales Brucknerfest, Linzer Klangwolke (September), Ars Electronica, Sommertheater im Schlosshof, Arkadenkonzerte im Linzer Landhaus (during the summer), Urfahrer Jahrmarkt, Linz-Fest, Pflasterspektakel

Theatre
Linzer Landestheater (Großes Haus and Kammerspiele), Theaterkeller im Kulturzentrum Ursulinenhof, Linzer Kellertheater (Hauptplatz 33), Kinderkulturzentrum Kuddelmuddel (former Kolpingkino, Langgasse 13), Posthof – Contemporary Culture on the Waterfront, Theater Phönix, Offenes Kulturhaus

Baths and Bathing lakes
Experience baths of Hummelhof and Schörgenhub, Parkbad, Pichlinger See, Pleschinger See (partly FKK), Feldkirchner Seen, Weiklersee (FKK)

Airport
Linz Hörsching

Places of Interest near Linz
Pöstlingberg (Wallfahrtsbasilika and Märchengrottenbahn), Stift Wilhering, Kürnberger Wald, Stift St. Florian, Schloss Hohenbrunn, Tillysburg, Lichtenberg, Pesenbachtal, Hellmonsödt, Kirchschlag, Pferdeeisenbahnpromenade, Ansfelden (Bruckner-Geburtshaus), Lauriacum (Lorch), Kefermarkt (Altar, Schloss Weinberg), Danube Valley and Danube bike trail

Die Farbabbildungen stammen von folgenden Photographen:
A. Andreß, Linz (Seiten 2 r.o., 3 l.o., 3 M., 4/5, 6, 7, 8/9, 12, 13, 22 l.u., 22 r.o., 24, 26, 30, 31, 32, 34, 35, 39 l.o., 39 r.u., 40 o., 40 u., 41, 42, 43, 44, 45, 46, 50, 51, 54, 55, 56 l.o., 56 r.u., 57, 58, 59, 60, 61, 64, 66 r.u., 67 o., 68, 70, 71, 72 l.o., 74, 75, 76 l.o., 76 l.u., 77, 83, 85, 86 l.o., 86 r.u., 87 l.u., 88 l.o., 88 l.u., 89, 90 o., 90 u., 91 o., 91 u., 92 o., 92 M., 92 u., 93, 94, 95, 96 o., 97, 100 l.o., 100 r.o., 100 u., 101, 102 l.o., 102 r.o., 102 u., 103 o., 103 u., 104, 105, 107, 108, 109, 110 o., 110 u., 111 o., 111 u., 111 r.u., 112 o., 114, 115, 116, 117, 118, 121, 124, 125 l.o., 125 r.o.); Archiv Chemie Linz (Seite 5 u., 79 o.); Archiv ESG, Linz (Seite 78); Archiv VOEST-ALPINE (Seiten 80 o., 80 u.); Archiv VOEST-ALPINE Industrieanlagenbau (Seite 82); Archiv VOEST-ALPINE M.C.E. (Seite 79 l.u.); Archiv VOEST-ALPINE Stahl (Seiten 79 r.u., 81 u.); Archiv Stift Wilhering (Seiten 119, 120); A. Aumayr, Linz (Seite 47); Foto Design Schaffler, Linz (Seite 63); W. Entlicher, Linz (Seiten 6 l.o., 18); F. Hubmann, Wien (Seiten 2 M., 2 r.u., 10, 11 l.o., 11 r.o., 11 l.u., 11 r.u., 14, 15, 19, 20, 21, 25 l., 25 r., 27, 29, 33 l., 33 r., 36 r., 37, 48 l.u., 49, 52, 72 u., 96 u., 99, 112 o., 123 l.o., 123 r.o.); E. Lessing, Wien (Seite 69); P. Peter, Linz (Seiten 3, 16, 17, 23, 36 l., 38 o., 38 u., 48 r.u., 62, 65, 66 o., 67 u., 72 l.u., 84, 87 o., 96 o., 97, 98, 106, 112 u., 113 o., 113 u.); W. Puchner, Wien (Seite 26 o.); G. Riha, Wien (Seite 87 r.u.); G. Trumler, Wien (Seiten 73, 122, 123 u.)

1. Auflage

Das Einband-Bild zeigt den Linzer Hauptplatz mit der Dreifaltigkeitssäule, im Hintergrund den Pöstlingberg.

Die graphische Gestaltung des Werkes, den Entwurf des Umschlages sowie die technische Betreuung besorgte Rudolf Metzger, das Lektorat Bettina Schiefer. Gesetzt wurde bei P. Kautzner in Wien. Die Reproduktion der Abbildungen, Druck und Bindung erfolgten bei C. & E. Grosser in Linz.

ISBN 3-85447-626-4

Christian Brandstätter Verlagsgesellschaft m.b.H.
A-1080 Wien, Wickenburggasse 26 · Telephon (++43-1) 408 38 14